CROSSING BOUNDARIES

Sharing God's Good News
through Mission

DAVID W. SCOTT

Crossing Boundaries: Sharing God's Good News through Mission

The General Board of Higher Education and Ministry leads and serves The United Methodist Church in the recruitment, preparation, nurture, education, and support of Christian leaders—lay and clergy—for the work of making disciples of Jesus Christ for the transformation of the world. The General Board of Higher Education and Ministry of The United Methodist Church serves as an advocate for the intellectual life of the church. The Board's mission embodies the Wesleyan tradition of commitment to the education of laypersons and ordained persons by providing access to higher education for all persons.

Wesley's Foundery Books is named for the abandoned foundery that early followers of John Wesley transformed, which later became the cradle of London's Methodist movement.

HIGHER EDUCATION & MINISTRY
General Board of Higher Education and Ministry
THE UNITED METHODIST CHURCH

For those contexts that have shaped me:
Decorah, Lawrence, Boston, Ripon

Contents

Acknowledgments

I would first like to thank Thomas Kemper for permitting me to use some of my work time at Global Ministries on this book project. This book would not have happened without his support. I'd also like to thank Kathy Armistead of the General Board of Higher Education and Ministry for being an enthusiastic partner in publishing this book. Again, this book would not have happened without her support. In addition, Scott Parrish deserves credit for the genesis of this book, as the idea emerged out of a conversation I had with him.

Thanks also to those who read early versions of this book and provided feedback on them. Among them are colleagues from Global Ministries, including Jerome Sahabandhu, Nora Colmenares, Kathleen Masters, David Logeman, and Quest Hunter; my friend and colleague, Taylor Walters Denyer; and members of The Family Church, Neenah, Wisconsin, including Scott Challoner, Crystal Wheeler, Jen Olkowski, and Trina Haase. Thank you all for your suggestions, even when I have not taken them. Your feedback has certainly made this a better book.

I would like to thank the United Methodist Professors of Mission for nurturing me in my professional and intellectual development as a missiologist. Most of the ideas in this book originally come from conversations with members of the UMPM, especially

Dana Robert, Henk Pieterse, and Robert Hunt. I stand on the shoulders of giants here.

Finally, thanks to my wife, Allie Scott, not just for being a generally fantastic and supportive spouse but also for helping in some very specific ways with this book—talking through ideas, providing reading suggestions, organizing feedback on the book. I'm so grateful to be in mission together with you.

Introduction

Do any of the following experiences with mission sound familiar to you?

- Once a month, people from your congregation serve a meal at the local homeless shelter. Some people really seem to enjoy going, but there's never quite enough of these people to fill up the required number of slots. Many people think that this program is a good idea in principle but seem unwilling to make room in their busy schedules to participate themselves. So, the woman who organizes this program is always badgering others in the congregation to sign up. Somehow, she always manages to find enough people, but it also always seems like such an ordeal. Is it really worth it?

- One of the major responsibilities for your church's mission committee is giving money to local religious and nonprofit organizations. The committee is reviewing this year's allocations. The church has always given $1,000 to a local children's services organization, but nobody seems to remember why the church started giving that money or even when. Nor is anyone really certain what the organization does with the money. Surely, it's something good, but what exactly? How important is it to continue to give that $1,000 to this organization? Could it be better used somewhere else?

■ Your church has a yearly youth mission trip. Every summer, you load up a couple of 15-passenger vans and drive down to fix homes in Appalachia. Everyone who goes always has a great time, both the youth and the adult leaders. The participants enjoy working together, camping out in the guest house together, singing songs, and playing games together. There's always a sense of accomplishment when they see how much they've done at the end of the week, and on the last day, it's traditional to go to the nearby waterpark, where everyone has a blast. There's such a high of being on the trip, but once everyone gets back home, that high quickly wears off. People go back to their normal lives, and some of the high schoolers who go on trips don't even come to church anymore by the time of the next trip. And there are always more houses to fix the next year. The area to which your church goes never seems to really improve. What is really being accomplished by these trips?

■ Your church has an annual international mission trip to a different location each year, but usually to somewhere warm and tropical to build buildings and distribute supplies to the poor. Participants always come back with great pictures of smiling children and gorgeous scenery. They tell stories about how happy and content the people are, despite their poverty. But if they are already happy and content, how are these trips really improving their lives? How is it even possible to know the long-term impacts of these trips when your church never returns to the same place twice?

My sense is that these four stories will sound familiar to many American United Methodists (and other American Christians). They represent four common ways in which local churches think about mission. Maybe your church participates in one of these types of activities, maybe it participates in all of them.

I hope not only that the stories resonate with you, but that you found the questions at the end of each one provocative as well. They get at an important central issue: Are we doing the right things in our mission activities? Generally, people have the sense that the programs and projects they do for mission are generally "good" things to do, but that may still leave them with uncertainties about the impact of their activities and how important those activities are, especially in the face of a slew of competing options. While few Christians doubt that it is theoretically a good idea to be involved in mission, it can often seem like an optional add-on to the life of the church, something to be done once the bills are paid and the committee work is taken care of. Even when churches do engage in mission, it can seem like there's no real outcome to it beyond the good feeling the participants get from helping others.

But what if that didn't have to be the case? What if it was possible to understand mission in a new way, not as a program that involves helping, but as a central aspect of what it means to be a Christian, to experience God's good news in our lives, and to respond to Christ's call on our lives? What if we could stop focusing on *doing* programs and start focusing on *being* the Body of Christ and *loving* God and others. What if we could open ourselves to the power of the Holy Spirit to transform our churches, our communities, and the world?

If these "what ifs" excite you, then this is the book for you.

About This Book

The goals of this book are practical: To help you and your church think about mission in new and deeper ways so that you can engage in mission with confidence and clarity, experience the spiritual benefits of joining in God's mission in the world, and serve God and others more effectively. The book presents a vision of mission that draws on both Wesleyan theology and ecumenical thinking about mission. Yet the goal is to do more than just present a theology of mission but rather to make suggestions about how to use this theology to shape or reshape your and your congregation's mission work. Thus, theology is mixed with suggestions for practice, and additional aids at the end of each chapter help readers apply the concepts discussed.

A series of discussion questions at the end of each chapter is intended to serve as the basis for group study. My hope is that this book could be used as a six-week study by your mission committee, Administrative Council, youth group, Sunday school class, United Methodist Women or United Methodist Men gatherings, or other church groups. The study questions are designed to help you reflect on your current mission work.

Each chapter also includes a list of further readings and resources for those interested in learning more about related topics. This list of readings is annotated, with brief descriptions of the materials, to help you select which ones will be most helpful to you in your further learning about and growth in mission.

Of course, I cannot tell you exactly how your church should be in mission in the world. I don't know all of the specifics of your congregation and the mission work you have engaged in or hope to engage in. Nor should you allow one person, whether that is me or anyone else, to make all of the decisions about your congregation's mission work. Congregational mission is a product of congregational discernment. I can, however, help guide you into conversations that can help you discern where God is calling you. Thus, this book is intended as an invitation to engage in conversation. First, it's an invitation to engage in conversation with me as the author and with the ideas I present in this book. If you'd like to respond directly, please do so via Twitter (@davidwmscott) and via the blog about mission that I curate, *UM & Global* (www .umglobal.org). Second, it's an invitation to engage in conversation with each other as Christian brothers and sisters and with people in the communities with whom you are in mission. It's an invitation to talk with each other about how exactly to apply the ideas from this book.

Conversation is actually an important concept for this book. Chapter 1 will suggest and then unpack a definition for mission: mission is cultivating relationships across boundaries for the sake of fostering conversations in word and deed about the nature of God's good news. It then connects this practice of mission to the broader life of faith. Chapter 2 will examine how such an understanding of mission can help us re-read one of Jesus's most important parables: the parable of the good Samaritan. Chapters 3 through 6 examine components of this definition in greater depth. Chapter 3 looks at biblical meanings of good news. Chapter 4 makes the case for relationships as central to mission and emphasizes the importance of these relationships crossing boundaries. Chapter 5 explores the significance of these boundaries for how we form relationships and engage in conversation with one another. Chapter 6 presents a vision of what it looks like to have conversations about God's good news in the context of these cross-boundary relationships.

The understanding of mission presented in this book is significantly different than how the church has traditionally thought about it. Those differences may challenge you. I hope they do at points. But even when they're challenging, I hope you take them seriously, and I hope they lead to some good conversations about mission. My dad used to have a weekly comment on the radio. One of his listeners once told him, "You may not always be right, but you sure do stir the pot." Whether or not you think I'm always right in what I say in this book, I hope it stirs the pot for you and gets the conversation going.

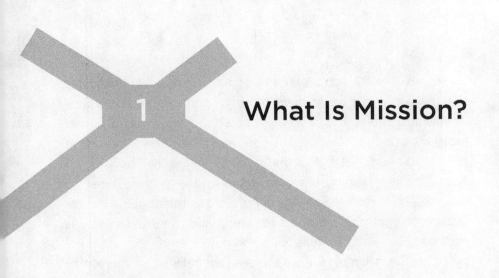

What Is Mission?

*Jesus said to them again, "Peace be with you. As the Father
sent me, so I am sending you." (John 20:21 CEB)*

Mission and Helping

My guess is that if you asked the average person in a pew on
Sunday morning, they would not have a definition of mission that
they could rattle off to you. While some Christians are deeply
committed to mission and have thought extensively about it,
many Christians have not thought about mission enough to have
a pat definition ready-to-hand. But I would further guess that if
you pushed that hypothetical average parishioner to come up
with a definition of mission, it would be something along the lines
of "helping others." Mission as helping is a common basic understanding across many churches, and for good reason. The Bible
is full of passages such as Matthew 25:31-46, which encourage
the followers of Jesus to show compassion and care for others
by feeding the hungry, giving water to the thirsty, welcoming the
stranger, clothing the naked, caring for the sick, and visiting those
in prison.

1

To say that mission is primarily about helping others indicates that mission involves Christians providing some sort of assistance or something of value to other people, who are in need of that assistance or item of value. Thus, it presumes that we, the Christians in mission, are the "haves," and others are the "have-nots." Not all forms of helping, then, are recognized as mission. If we give a homeless person a blanket, that is seen as mission; if a homeless person helps us change a flat tire, that is not usually seen as mission, even if the homeless person does it as an expression of his or her Christian faith. If we share a spiritual insight with someone else, that is mission in the form of evangelism, but if we get a spiritual insight from someone else, that is a "God moment." If we define mission as helping, it usually involves an unspoken sense of who is doing the helping—us!

Christians also often interpret mission as helping in programmatic ways. If you asked your average worshipper what they meant by "mission is helping others," they would probably give you examples of programs that their church carries out to help others—a soup kitchen, a toy distribution drive, trips to other countries to paint schools, etc. Perhaps this definition would also include evangelism, in which we help others come to the Christian faith, often by following a particular script or program for presenting the faith. In all four vignettes in the introduction, mission is presented as a program activity that involves helping others.

To say that mission is a program indicates that it is something that happens at specified times and places in an organized fashion. Whether that takes the form of a mission trip, a service project, or a financial transaction, there is an identifiable and planned action or set of actions, often with formal responsibilities, budgets, a sponsoring organization, etc., that can be termed "mission." Thinking of mission as a program also involves making distinctions between what types of helping count as mission and what do not. If we move furniture because a friend is changing apartments, that is not seen as mission; if we move furniture because our church is holding a rummage sale where the proceeds go to the food pantry, that is seen as mission. The action is the same, but one is an informal act of helping and one is an organized, formal program of helping. It's the organized, formal program that is counted as mission.

I do not want to suggest that helping or formal programs are necessarily and always bad, but I would like to point out that this understanding of mission is limited and potentially problematic as well. Thinking of mission as helping programs is limited, because it makes us miss the breadth of God's mission in the world and the full spiritual significance of joining in that mission. Many Christians would say that we should help others because God calls us to love others. That is true: God does call us to love others. Yet to equate helping and love is to dramatically misunderstand love, both God's and ours. Helping may be part of love, but it cannot be the entirety of love.

> **Helping may be part of love, but it's not the whole.**

Take as an illustration love as expressed in a marriage. One of my "love languages" in my marriage is doing things for my wife—in other words, helping.[1] Sometimes she really appreciates my help. When she comes home from a work trip and the house is picked up, the laundry put away, the kids have both been bathed, and the lawn is mowed, that can be a big relief for her. Other times, I think I get more out of doing the helping than she does being helped. That experience also has mission parallels—oftentimes our mission is more about how we feel than the impact on our mission partners.

Yet even when my wife appreciates my help, if helping was the only way I ever showed my love to her, if I never said I loved her, never spent time with her, never gave her gifts, never touched her, I would be more like a handyman and maid than a husband to her.

---

1   Gary Chapman, *The Five Love Languages: How to Express Heartfelt Commitment to Your Mate* (Waterville, ME: Thorndike Press, 2005). Chapman's Love Language #4 is "acts of service," i.e., helping.

I know that she would not find that a satisfying expression of love and, ultimately, I know I would not either. While I enjoy doing acts of service for her, I know there's more to the relationship than that, and I want there to be more to the relationship than that.

While marriage is a special relationship, I think this insight applies to other forms of love as well. Others know that we love them not only because we serve them but because we spend time with them, share our treasures with them, and tell them how much they mean to us. Indeed, the ways we can show love to others go well beyond this list of "love languages" for romantic relationships. Love expressed through service is good, but it is not a complete love. To confine love to helping is a limited understanding of love. In the same way, seeing mission as helping gives a limited understanding of the love God has for us and the love God calls us to share with the world.

Our understanding of mission is especially limited if we think of helping only in programmatic terms. When we see mission as a program, then we limit it to only those times and those places where such programs occur. If mission is a program, then it cannot be a way of life. A way of life happens at all times and in any place. When we limit mission to specific programs, then it becomes easier to see mission as a small or optional component of the Christian faith and not a central aspect of how we live out our Christian calling. Yet, mission properly understood should be central to how we understand and practice our faith. The end of this chapter will expand on this point significantly.

An understanding of mission as helping programs, though, is not only limited but actually harmful at times. Such an understanding is especially problematic when we see helping as always flowing from the "haves" (the Christians in our congregation or group) to the "have-nots" (everybody else). As books such as *When Helping Hurts* by Steve Corbett and Brian Fikkert[2] and

---

2   Steve Corbett and Brian Fikkert, *When Helping Hurts: How to Alleviate Poverty without Hurting the Poor . . . and Yourself* (Chicago: Moody Publishers, 2012).

Toxic Charity by Robert Lupton[3] show, it is quite possible to set out to help others but to actually have the opposite effect, if we do so with improper understandings and attitudes. As Corbett and Fikkert write, when we combine a material definition of poverty with a sense of the superiority of the materially nonpoor and a sense of the inferiority of the materially poor, then we end up doing harm—spiritually, emotionally, economically, and/or socially—to both the materially poor and the materially nonpoor.[4]

Reading resources such as *When Helping Hurts* and *Toxic Charity* is important to make sure we are helping in ways that are, well, helpful. Yet it is also important to develop a fuller and more robust understanding of mission that goes beyond just understanding mission as helping programs, especially since, as we have just seen, even when it is not harmful, such a definition is still limited. It is to such a fuller understanding of mission that we now turn.

Mission and Sending

Our term *mission* comes from a Latin word meaning "to send." While *mission* has only been used as a term to describe the activities of the Church and individual Christians for the past few centuries, *missio* as a verb meaning "to send" is all throughout the Bible. (At least in the Latin translation. In Greek, the original language of the New Testament, the term is *apostellein*. More about that word in a bit.)

One of the most important instances of sending in the Bible is God sending Jesus to be God incarnate among humans. The Gospel of John in particular strongly emphasizes God's role in sending Jesus. Throughout John, Jesus refers to God as "the one who sent me" or "the Father who sent me." Moreover, when Jesus mentions the Holy Spirit in the Gospel of John, he refers

---

3   Robert D. Lupton, *Toxic Charity: How Churches and Charities Hurt Those They Help (And How to Reverse It)* (New York: HarperOne, 2011).

4   Corbett and Fikkert, *When Helping Hurts*, 64.

to sending the Holy Spirit from the Father and himself. A biblical understanding of mission as sending thus starts with the Triune God sending Godself to the world, especially in the form of God the Parent sending Jesus into the world and God the Parent and Jesus together sending the Holy Spirit into the world.

Yet the biblical understanding of sending doesn't stop with Jesus and the Holy Spirit. As the verse from John at the start of this chapter indicates, Jesus sends his followers too. In his first post-Resurrection interaction with his disciples, Jesus says, "As the Father sent me, so I am sending you" (John 20:21). This is actually the second time in the Gospel of John that Jesus mentions sending the disciples. In Jesus's prayer at the Last Supper, he says of the disciples, "As you sent me into the world, so I have sent them into the world" (John 17:18). It is clear that the disciples being sent in mission by Jesus parallels the way in which God sent Jesus in mission.

This sending of disciples by Jesus also echoes the sending of prophets by God in the Old Testament. Moses (Exodus 3:10), Isaiah (Isaiah 6:8), Jeremiah (Jeremiah 1:7), and Ezekiel (Ezekiel 2:3-4) all experienced their calling to serve God as a calling to be sent. God sent these prophets "to the Israelites," as Ezekiel puts it, just as Jesus sent his disciples "into the world." Both prophets and disciples are sent by God to a group of people.

Thus, as Christians, our participation in mission starts with our answering Jesus's call on our lives. Jesus's call is both a call to "follow me" (Jesus's repeated invitation to many of his disciples throughout the gospels) and a call to "therefore, go" (Matthew 28:19). When we answer yes to Jesus's call, we are saying yes not only to walking with him but also yes to being sent out by him to others.

God is the sender; we are the sent.

It is important to emphasize that, in mission, both the Church and individual Christians are the sent, not the senders. God is the sender, and God ultimately

6

starts, owns, and controls mission (a concept that missiologists, those who study mission, call the *missio Dei*). As Christians, God calls us to participate in God's mission, which we do not start, own, or control. God sends us; we do not send ourselves. Thus, true mission must be grounded in God's love for the world, not any of our own desires.

Mission in Motion

Note that all three terms used above for God's call—following, going, being sent—imply movement. As my former pastor (and later bishop) Martin McLee used to say, the Christian faith is a journey. And since the Christian life involves movement and being on a journey, it must also involve crossing boundaries. Movement is about change, and boundaries mark the transition from one thing to another. Without crossing any boundaries, there can be no movement. We cannot go anywhere on our journeys if we cross no boundaries.

Boundaries are lines that separate different areas or concepts. Boundaries can be distinct and sharp, like the boundaries that separate states. When driving in a car, you can point out the window to the sign that says, "Welcome to Illinois," and you will know you have crossed a state boundary. Boundaries can also be gradual. When driving, you can tell when you are driving through plains and when you are driving in the mountains, but you may not be able to point out the exact moment when you crossed from one to the other with the same precision as you can point to the sign for the state border.

Boundaries can be physical boundaries, as the two examples above show, but there are many more types of boundaries as well. Many boundaries divide different groups of people— age, gender, class, nationality, race, ethnicity, tribe, religion, political affiliation, language, culture, etc. Other boundaries mark different concepts—sacred/profane, clean/unclean, feminine/masculine, formal/informal, urban/rural, Christian/

un-Christian, etc. These human and conceptual boundaries can also be sharp or gradual.

Jesus himself crossed boundaries in his mission of being sent by the Father. In the Incarnation, he crossed the boundary between heaven and earth, between divine and human. In his ministry, he walked around, frequently crossing the political boundaries of the time that divided Galilee, Judea, and surrounding territories. He crossed social boundaries that divided Pharisees from tax collectors and sinners, as well as Jews from Samaritans and Syrophoenicians. He ministered to men, women, and children. In his crucifixion and resurrection, he crossed the boundary from life to death—and then crossed back!

> To be in mission involves crossing boundaries, especially those that divide people from one another.

To be a Christian in mission, then, involves crossing boundaries, especially across the boundaries that divide people from one another. Jesus may or may not send us across physical and geographic boundaries. Mission can happen within our own local communities, within our own home countries, and across the world. But wherever it happens, mission must involve crossing boundaries that divide us from other humans. Chapters 4 and 5 will discuss in much greater depth what is involved in crossing such boundaries. But for now, know that unless we cross such boundaries, we have not fully been sent by God; we are not truly in mission.

The Message and the Messengers

We have seen that mission involves being sent across boundaries by God. But to what end? Why are we sent, and what are we supposed to do once we have crossed boundaries? To gain some insight into the answer to these questions, let's turn again to examine biblical models of sending.

Often when the term "send" is used in the New Testament, it is used to describe someone sending a message to someone else. Such messages can range from the mundane to the eternally significant, but it is clear that one of the primary things that people *send* in the Bible is messages. In the Gospel of Luke, Jesus refers to his own ministry in terms of being sent with a message. In Luke 4, he describes his ministry by quoting the prophet Isaiah, saying:

The Spirit of the Lord is upon me,
    because the Lord has anointed me.
He has sent me to preach good news to the poor,
    to proclaim release to the prisoners
    and recovery of sight to the blind,
    to liberate the oppressed,
    and to proclaim the year of the Lord's favor.
    (Luke 4:18-19)

Shortly after, Jesus again refers to his ministry by saying, "I must preach the good news of God's kingdom in other cities too, for this is why I was sent" (Luke 4: 43). The words "preach" and "proclaim" indicate that Jesus understood himself as having a message to convey to others.

In both of these instances, Jesus refers to his message as "good news." This concept of good news is central to Christianity. The term *gospel* comes from "good news." So, too, does the term "evangelism." Chapter 3 will go into much more depth on this subject. As Christians, we think of ourselves as people who have received good news and thus have good news to share with others. Jesus was sent with good news for the world, and since we are sent in the same manner as Jesus, we too are sent with good news for the world. When Jesus commissions his disciples in mission in John 20, it is just after they have received the best news possible—Jesus is not dead but has risen! To be in mission involves having good news.

Yet throughout the New Testament, it is not just messages that get sent, but messengers. John's disciples and the Pharisees send messengers to Jesus. The early Christian communities send messengers between each other. And Jesus sends his disciples as messengers. In fact, the term "apostle" comes from the Greek word for messenger. The apostles are Jesus's messengers in the world.

It's important to understand that in the New Testament, messengers were more than just mail carriers. They were representatives of the one who sent them. They did more than simply relay a string of words; they dialogued with others on behalf of the sender. They engaged those to whom they were sent in unscripted (or not fully scripted) communication. In so doing, they had to understand the will, values, and interests of the one who sent them and be able to represent those to the best of their ability in dynamic situations. Messages weren't unidirectional proclamation; they were conveyed through interaction and conversation. A good messenger was one who could faithfully represent the point of view of the person(s) who sent them and communicate it effectively in a conversation with someone else.

The primary distinction between proclamation and conversation is that proclamation is one-sided while conversation is two-sided. The two-sided nature of conversation is essential for communication. It is possible to hear something without understanding (something Jesus knew well [Matthew 13:13-14]). Conversation allows for the one hearing the message to ask questions, to clarify, to push back, to connect the message to their own knowledge and understandings. It is much easier just to proclaim in a one-sided fashion, but for the fullest communication to happen, it is important to be able to engage in conversation. Thus, being a messenger could be a complex and significant task, to fully communicate someone else's message through conversation with another.

Conversation, Credibility, and Connection

Moreover, a messenger would only be a credible representative of someone in a conversation if they were acting in accord with what the other person in the conversation knew about the will, values, and interests of the one who sent them. If either Jesus's disciples or the Pharisees' disciples had worn symbols of Roman gods, no one would have believed that they came as real representatives of their Jewish teachers. Thus, the disciples were representatives of Jesus and his message who lived in accordance with that message, not just people who repeated Jesus's exact words to others.

A related concept with a similar dual meaning is the term "witness." The Book of Acts frequently mentions being a witness for Jesus and testifying on his behalf (the word "testify" comes from the Greek word for "witness," as does the word "testament"). A witness can both give evidence of something and *be themselves* evidence of that thing. Jesus both gave us evidence of the good news of God's love through his teaching and was himself the evidence of that good news through his ministry, death, and resurrection. When Jesus sent his disciples as his messengers, he was expecting them to witness through the evidence of their lives to the truth of his message.

> **To act as God's messengers, our lives must be part of that message.**

In a similar way, for us to act as true messengers, true witnesses, for Jesus, it is necessary that our lives be part of that message. The consistency between our lives and our words helps establish the credibility and authenticity of our message. Yet, our lives cannot be witness to the credibility of our message unless others are familiar with them. People become familiar with our lives through the process of forming relationships with us. It is relationships that allow for our lives and actions to fulfill their part in our witness.

Therefore, the best mission involves conversations carried out as part of ongoing relationships. It is only within conversation that messages can fully be conveyed, clarified, and communicated. It is only within the context of relationship that we can demonstrate love so that our lives can speak their part of the message of God's good news. Thus, relationship and conversation are both necessary for us to be witnesses for and witnesses of God's good news.

A New Definition of Mission

Putting together what we've seen of mission thus far, it is finally possible to offer a definition of mission that goes beyond "helping programs." Following the biblical precedents we have seen in this chapter, mission can be defined as cultivating relationships across boundaries for the sake of fostering conversations in word and deed about the nature of God's good news. This is a long definition, so we'll unpack it by looking at the four main parts of this definition.

> Mission is cultivating relationships across boundaries for the sake of fostering conversations in word and deed about God's good news.

First, mission involves good news. As we saw in our discussion of the biblical roots of the term mission, those who are sent are sent with a message. That message is good news. This is what makes Christian mission distinctively Christian as opposed to other forms of boundary-crossing collaboration, such as international nongovernmental work, political diplomacy, transnational business, or global cultural phenomena. Note that it's not just evangelism that involves good news. All forms of mission should have a component of good news to them. They should be both good and involve something new or not present in that situation before. Thus, good news is not just a narrow formulation of theology but includes the full breadth of God's good actions in the world. Chapter 3 will explore the nature of this good news in greater detail.

Second, mission involves relationship. We saw above that messengers are most credible when they act and live in ways that are consistent with their message, and it is relationship that best allows others to judge our consistency, authenticity, and, therefore, credibility. Moreover, as chapter 3 will show, relationship is a primary form of good news tied to other forms of good news. Mission is less about doing and more about being in relationship with others. Chapter 4 will explore the importance of relationship to mission more fully.

Third, mission involves crossing boundaries. As the biblical discussion of mission above showed, mission involves being sent across human boundaries. Mission involves something more than just relating to those we already know who are like us in almost every way. It involves encountering the Other. Chapter 5 will discuss the importance of differences and boundary crossing in mission.

Fourth and finally, mission involves conversations in word and deed. Mission involves cultivating relationships across boundaries not just for their own sakes, but for the sake of understanding the good news. Yet understanding that good news is a mutual process. It involves conversations between all mission partners, and between humans, the Bible, and human contexts. It is a process of mutual learning, not a monologue in which we seek to unload our information on others. While words are a central medium by which we have conversations, actions also have their place in mission as a way of demonstrating our understandings of good news and observing others' understandings. Chapter 6 will discuss this process of conversation.

It is important to include a note about terminology regarding those involved in mission. While the Western church has traditionally thought of missionaries as those sent in mission, this book is intended for all Christians, since we are all sent out in mission. Yet mission, especially when we conceive of it as relationship, involves more than just those being sent. It also involves others whom they encounter as they go. These others may also be Christians and may also be sent out on their own mission journeys. In other instances, these others may be non-Christians of a variety of faith backgrounds or none. When we engage in mission, we encounter many people, form relationships with some of them, and work cooperatively with some of those. Thus, this book uses a couple of terms to describe those we meet in our mission journeys. This book uses the admittedly clunky phrase "those among whom we are in mission" to describe the whole range of people we encounter, whether or not we have relationships with them. It also uses the term "mission partners" to describe those with whom we have (or are developing) relationships, including those with whom we work jointly.

Varieties of Mission Work

This definition of mission as cultivating relationships across boundaries for the sake of fostering conversations in word and deed about the nature of God's good news is biblically grounded and more complex than a definition of mission as helping programs, but it's also more abstract. Yet the goal of this book is to provide practical help, not just theological abstractions! Therefore, it's important to think about how this definition of mission connects with the actual types of mission in which people engage.

Mission is a broad category of Christian activity, and scholars and church leaders have identified several different types of activities under the umbrella of mission. One such list is the the Five Marks of Mission:

1. To proclaim the Good News of the kingdom
2. To teach, baptize, and nurture new believers
3. To respond to human need by loving service
4. To seek to transform unjust structures of society

5. To strive to safeguard the integrity of creation and sustain and renew the life of the earth[5]

The Five Marks are a widely used categorization of mission activities that come out of a Church of England background. In *Mission in the 21st Century: Exploring the Five Marks of Global Mission*, Andrew Walls and Cathy Ross acknowledge, "The Five Marks are neither a perfect nor a complete definition of mission . . . However, they are also rich with potential and they do form a good working basis for a holistic approach to mission."[6]

The value of such a list of the types of mission is that it helps us be clear about the differences between varying aspects of mission in a way that avoids conflating them. Such clarity helps prevent confusion among all those involved in mission work, both those sent in mission and their partners. At the same time, such lists also make it possible to see how different aspects of mission are related to one another. Tracing such connections can involve looking for points of intersection between activities as well as identifying how all activities stem from a common understanding of mission, both of which contribute to the sort of holistic understanding Walls and Ross emphasize.

The first category, "to proclaim the Good News of the kingdom," has traditionally been understood as entailing evangelism. The connection of this category to this book's definition of mission is perhaps obvious, centering as they both do on good news. Evangelism involves beginning the conversation about God's good news with those who were previously unfamiliar with it, or at least unfamiliar with the Christian understanding of God's good news. Because of God's prevenient grace in the world, we may expect all people to have some prior experience of God's good news, whether or not they recognize it as such. The goal of

---

5   From Andrew Walls and Cathy Ross, eds. *Mission in the 21st Century: Exploring the Five Marks of Global Mission* (Maryknoll, NY: Orbis Books, 2008), xiv.

6   Walls and Ross, *Mission in the 21st Century,* xiv.

evangelism is to help others recognize God's good news as coming from God through Christ.

While the wording of this Mark in Walls and Ross does use the word "proclaim," that does not mean that they (or anyone else using the Five Marks) take a one-sided approach to evangelism that involves talking at others instead of talking *with* them. Evangelism is entirely compatible with the sort of conversational, relational understanding of mission put forward above. Indeed, many have written about how evangelism is most effective within the context of ongoing relationships and how for the gospel to become fully rooted in a new culture, it must be the result of an ongoing conversation.[7]

The second of the Five Marks, "to teach, baptize, and nurture new believers," recognizes that the conversation about God's good news does not stop once someone has made some sort of initial decision to become a Christian. One could say that the process of discussing and understanding God's good news is part of the lifelong process of discipleship for all Christians. (Indeed, I'll say that very thing below.) Hence, while new believers may be the ones being baptized, it is not just new believers who are taught about and nurtured by the good news. Moreover, if the life of faith involves growing in understanding of God's good news, then it is not just those who have been believers longer who teach those who have been believers for a shorter amount of time. As representatives of and messengers from God in Christ, all Christians have a piece of God's message to share with others.

Such an affirmation of the importance of being in conversation about God's good news with other believers is especially important for global, multicultural denominations such as The United Methodist Church. Mission can involve cross-cultural conversations whereby all believers share their understandings

---

7   One recent Methodist example of such an approach to evangelism is Henry H. Knight III and F. Douglas Powe Jr.'s *Transforming Evangelism: The Wesleyan Way of Sharing Faith* (Nashville: Discipleship Resources, 2006).

of God's good news and listen to the insights into that good news that our fellow Christians from other backgrounds have for us.

There are many ways "to respond to human need by loving service," as the Third Mark indicates. These ways include disaster relief, medical care, education, economic development, poverty relief, along with other forms of service. This category of mission work is perhaps the most similar to a traditional "helping programs" understanding of mission. Yet our new definition of mission fits here, too. Such service often occurs across human (and geographic) boundaries. It entails good news in at least two ways: first, the good news of service in the midst of one's need, but even more importantly the good news of the love that motivates the service—both the human love of those providing the service and, ultimately, God's love. This love is most effectively conveyed when such service is not just a one-off experience but part of longer, ongoing relationships that foster mutuality and give-and-take discussion of the nature and quality of that service.

While chapter 3 will have more to say about this, seeking "to transform unjust structures of society" can be quite good news to those oppressed by such unjust structures! The kingdoms of the world are not the kingdom of God. Sin, both personal and systemic, still characterizes all worldly kingdoms. Thus, to engage in conversations about the good news of God's kingdom is also to point out where worldly kingdoms offer bad news to their inhabitants and others. This bad news can take many forms: war, exploitation, neglect, violence, sexism, racism, tribalism, contempt for the poor, etc. Seeking to transform unjust societies is thus to share the good news that God opposes such instruments of suffering and oppression.

God's kingdom is a kingdom of peace, not just in the sense of the absence of war, but in the sense of deep well-being for all involved, what some call "peace with justice." God's desire that humans live in such a state of peace is an expression of God's love for humankind, love that is at the heart of God's good news. Jesus's teachings and redemptive death and resurrection and the Holy Spirit's regenerative work in our souls are important means by which God moves us toward this peace with justice. Such a state of collective and individual well-being, however, cannot be achieved in the absence of peaceful relationships with one another and ongoing conversations about what that well-being looks like. Relationships and conversations are especially important across the human boundaries that so often divide and become the pretext for oppression, violence, and war.

The fifth of the Five Marks, "to strive to safeguard the integrity of creation and sustain and renew the life of the earth," acknowledges that God's good news is not just good news for humanity but for all of God's creation. God fashioned the natural world and called it good before human sin marred that creation. God's redemptive plan for the universe is not just to restore and redeem humanity, but all that God has made. God promises "a new heaven and a new earth" (Revelation 21; Isaiah 66) that includes plants, animals, and natural features such as water. John Wesley's Sermon 60, "The General Deliverance," makes the argument for God's redemptive intention for all creation. Wesley writes, "I doubt not that the Father of All has a tender regard for even his lowest creatures, and that, in consequence of this, he will make them large amends for all they suffer while under their present bondage."[8]

If part of God's good news is good news for the created world, then Christians as messengers of God must testify to this aspect of good news as well. As God's sent representatives, we should act out God's love for all creation. Given the scale of the environmental challenges facing our planet today, we cannot hope to be effective in acting out such love without working in conversation and relationship with others, especially across geographic and political boundaries.

---

8   John Wesley, "Sermon 60: The General Deliverance," Wesley Center Online, http://wesley.nnu.edu/john-wesley/the-sermons-of-john-wesley-1872-edition/sermon-60-the-general-deliverance/, accessed July 24, 2018.

Much more could be said about any one of these areas of mission. More could be said about how an understanding of mission as cultivating relationships across boundaries for the sake of fostering conversations in word and deed about the nature of God's good news informs our theological understanding of each type of mission. More could be said about how congregations and broader Christian bodies can live out God's sending call in each of these types of mission. Unfortunately, there is not the space to do so here.

> **Mission is the heart of discipleship.**

Yet it is worthwhile keeping in mind the scope of God's mission before going further in our discussion. The goal of this book is not to persuade you that mission must look like one specific activity. Instead, I want to affirm the many types of mission work in which congregations are engaged. If your church is engaged in evangelism, good! If your church is engaged in justice-seeking mission, good! If your church is engaged in disaster recovery, good! Whatever type of mission you are engaged in, I hope you will continue to do it, while reassessing and refining your efforts in the light of any insights you gain from this book. I hope that readers will be drawn deeper into their own individual callings in mission from God while recognizing the many ways in which God calls others, too. As 1 Corinthians 12:4-6 says, "There are different spiritual gifts but the same Spirit; and there are different ministries and the same Lord; and there are different activities but the same God who produces all of them in everyone." Use the distinctive gifts that God has given you and your group for mission and encourage others to do the same.

Mission and the Christian Life

Whatever type of mission we engage in, it is important to remember that mission is not just a program we choose to participate in or an optional add-on to the Christian life; it is at the very heart of Christian discipleship. Mission is not just about helping others so that we can feel good about having been kind. It is living out central components of our Christian faith.

All too often, Christians think that being a Christian merely involves going to church, engaging in a couple of devotional practices, and living by a few moral rules. Worship and discipleship are indeed important parts of the Christian faith. Yet just as worship and discipleship are responses to our experience of the good news of God's love, so too is our participation in God's mission. When Jesus called his followers to "come and follow me," he was inviting them not just to go to a church service or to participate in a Bible study. He was inviting them to join in his ministry. He invited them to become part of God's mission of redemption and restoration in the world. As noted above, Jesus called his followers to both follow and be sent.

God still makes this same call to us today. It is true that God wants us to participate in communal worship and to engage in a variety of forms of discipleship. Yet God calls us to more as Christians. As with Jesus's call to his followers, God calls us to join in God's mission of redemption and restoration in the world. Without hearing and responding to that part of the call, we have missed the full meaning of God's message to us. We are not living the fullness of the Christian life.

Yet when we do hear and answer God's call to join in God's mission, we become fully Christian, not just in our beliefs or our religious practices, but in our relationship with the world. We become God's witnesses in the world, sent to converse about God's message of good news to the world. By so doing, we open ourselves to continued growth in our knowledge and love of God and others.

In this way, our mission feeds back into our discipleship. The Latin root upon which the English word "discipleship" is based is *discere*, which means "to learn." Disciples of Jesus are not just those who give their allegiance to Jesus or those who seek to do what Jesus instructs. They are apprentices of Jesus. They learn to engage in the same sort of work Jesus does. Thus, disciples look to see what Jesus is doing. Some of this happens through Bible study and prayer. This type of discipleship can equip us to be in mission. Yet we also see what Jesus is doing through engaging in mission. We are sent just as Jesus was sent and being in mission helps us to understand Jesus better. Mission is thus part of discipleship, and what we learn from mission will affect how we read the Bible and how we pray. In this way, discipleship is both grounds for and fruit of mission.

In a similar way, when we come to learn more of God's goodness through our missional discipleship, that learning is sure to overflow into worship. Worship can remind us of the good news of God's love in a way that strengthens and prepares us for mission. Yet, it also allows us to express our joy and gratitude for the evidence of God's love that we have discovered while engaged in mission. Thus, like discipleship, worship is both grounds for and fruit of mission.

When we come to see mission as a central component of our Christian faith and intimately connected to discipleship and worship, the other central components of our Christian faith, that is when we know that we are doing mission right. That is when mission can best transform us and the world around us. That is when mission connects us most deeply to the power of the Holy Spirit. That is when mission becomes a source of life for us and the world around us. And when that happens, it is truly good news! May you experience that good news in your life and the life of your church.

■ MISSION TAKEAWAYS

This chapter has covered a lot of ground theologically and biblically. What is most important to remember about the definition of mission? What concepts are crucial to understanding further chapters and your own church's mission work? We can identify three takeaways:

1. Mission is not just helping programs. Such a definition is at best a limited understanding of mission and at worst can lead to harm done in mission.
2. Mission can be understood as cultivating relationships across boundaries for the sake of fostering conversations in word and deed about the nature of God's good news. Mission involves being sent across human, and possibly geographic, boundaries by God. It involves being messengers and witnesses of God's good news. That good news is best communicated via mutual conversations that take place as part of ongoing relationships.
3. Within this broad definition, mission can take many forms. Included among these forms are evangelism, discipleship, service, peacebuilding and justice seeking, and care of creation. Yet, whatever form it takes, we should see mission as an intrinsic part of the life of Christian faith.

■ DISCUSSION QUESTIONS

Use these questions to guide group study of this chapter or for individual reflection:

1. Share a time when someone reached out and helped you in a significant way. What was it like? Did it change your relationship with that person? How?
2. Share a time when you or your church was in mission. What was it like? In what ways was it similar to a time someone helped you? In what ways was it different?
3. How would you define mission? How do you think others in your church would define mission? Why do we need a definition of mission?
4. Think about some of the current mission work that your church does. What have been the short- and long-term benefits?

5. Do you agree that seeing mission as helping is "at best limited and at worst harmful"? Why or why not? Can someone be too helpful? Give an example.
6. What do you think of the definition of mission as "cultivating relationships across boundaries for the sake of fostering conversations in word and deed about the nature of God's good news"? What are the connections between this definition and the current mission work of your congregation?
7. Give some examples of boundaries. What are boundaries that you face? What boundaries have you crossed in your Christian journey? What relationships have you developed in the process? What did you learn about God through these relationships? Are there boundaries that should never be crossed?
8. How can the Five Marks of Mission help us think about the different types of mission? Thinking about your own church's mission work, how do you see it fitting within these Five Marks?
9. In your opinion, why is mission at the heart of Christian faith? Why must Christians engage in mission? What are the benefits to the person, the church in mission?
10. Where do you believe God is calling you to go in mission? Where is God calling your church to go in mission?

■ FURTHER READING

Here are some other books related to topics in this chapter and why you should read them:

Steve Corbett and Brian Fikkert, *When Helping Hurts: How to Alleviate Poverty without Hurting the Poor . . . and Yourself* (Chicago: Moody Publishers, 2009). Corbett and Fikkert's book is the best warning out there of the dangers of traditional approaches that the well-to-do take to helping the poor. They frame their critique within a Christian theological view and make specific mentions of mission.

Jamie Wright, *The Very Worst Missionary: A Memoir or Whatever* (New York: Convergent Books, 2018). Frequently funny, often profane, and always honest, this spiritual autobiography relates Wright's experiences as a missionary in Costa Rica for five years. Wright critiques traditional models of short-term and long-term mission while affirming the importance of Christians loving their neighbors and God's ability to use even our misguided efforts to do good.

Samuel Wells, *A Nazareth Manifesto: Being with God* (Malden, MA: Wiley Blackwell, 2015). Wells argues for a shift from thinking of Christian mission as being primarily about "doing for" others to thinking of it as being primarily about "being with" others and God. Theological yet accessible, Wells's book presents a version of Christian theology, life, and ministry that flows from God being with us, us being with God, and us being with each other.

The United Methodist Church, *Grace Upon Grace: The Mission Statement of The United Methodist Church* (Nashville: Graded Press, 1990); and the *UM & Global* blog series evaluating *Grace Upon Grace*, "UM & Global," United Methodist Professors of Mission, 2013-14, www.umglobal. org/search/label/Grace%20Upon%20Grace. *Grace Upon Grace* is the UMC's official mission theology statement and therefore worth a read. The United Methodist Professors of Mission and others conducted a reassessment of it on the *UM & Global* blog twenty-five years after its initial publication.

The Good News and the Good Samaritan

"And who is my neighbor?" —Luke 10:29b

Mission and the Good Samaritan

As we explore the true meaning of mission, it is important to continue to look to the Bible for models that we can draw on. The Bible offers us many significant models for mission, including Jesus's initial commissioning of his disciples, the Great Commission, and the ministry of Paul. While these are all important passages with valuable insights into mission, I am going to explore another passage—the story of the good Samaritan.

There are several reasons to look at this passage. For many Christians, especially many American Christians, the story of the good Samaritan gets to the heart of how they understand and seek to live out their Christian faith. This story is a memorable and engaging one that reinforces one of the basic instructions of Christianity: Love your neighbor. Love for others is a key motivation for many Christians who engage in mission.

Yet Christians often interpret this command to love others in a particular way, as a command for those with wealth and power to go out and help the poor and less fortunate by giving food, clothing, medical care, etc. We see the story of the good Samaritan as justifying this understanding of loving as helping. By carefully rereading the story of the good Samaritan, we can reconsider some of our assumptions about what Christian love and mission really mean.

It also makes sense to read Luke's version of the parable of the good Samaritan as a parable that directly applies to mission. Luke, who is traditionally credited as being the author not only of the Gospel of Luke but also the Acts of the Apostles, is very interested in mission. The whole story arc of Luke and Acts can be read as a story not just about Jesus's life, teachings, death, and resurrection but as a story about God's mission to bring new life through Jesus, starting with Israel and then spreading to all the nations.

Not only is Luke generally interested in mission but the parable of the good Samaritan comes just after Jesus's commissioning of the seventy-two and their report on their mission work in the first part of Luke 10 (v. 1-24). The transition from the story of the seventy-two to the parable of the good Samaritan happens with the words "just then" (v. 25 NRSV). This immediate chronological linking shows that for Luke, the parable of the good Samaritan is directly connected to what came just before it. If the story of the commissioning of the seventy-two and their report back to Jesus is a story about mission, it makes sense then to consider the parable of the good Samaritan as a story about mission, too.

Here then, is the parable of the good Samaritan, as found in Luke 10:25-37 (CEB):

> A legal expert stood up to test Jesus. "Teacher," he said, "what must I do to gain eternal life?"
>
> Jesus replied, "What is written in the Law? How do you interpret it?"
>
> He responded, "You must love the Lord your God with all your heart, with all your being, with all your strength, and with all your mind, and love your neighbor as yourself."

Jesus said to him, "You have answered correctly. Do this and you will live."

But the legal expert wanted to prove that he was right, so he said to Jesus, "And who is my neighbor?"

Jesus replied, "A man went down from Jerusalem to Jericho. He encountered thieves, who stripped him naked, beat him up, and left him near death. Now it just so happened that a priest was also going down the same road. When he saw the injured man, he crossed over to the other side of the road and went on his way. Likewise, a Levite came by that spot, saw the injured man, and crossed over to the other side of the road and went on his way. A Samaritan, who was on a journey, came to where the man was. But when he saw him, he was moved with compassion. The Samaritan went to him and bandaged his wounds, tending them with oil and wine. Then he placed the wounded man on his own donkey, took him to an inn, and took care of him. The next day, he took two full days' worth of wages and gave them to the innkeeper. He said, 'Take care of him, and when I return, I will pay you back for any additional costs.' What do you think? Which one of these three was a neighbor to the man who encountered thieves?"

Then the legal expert said, "The one who demonstrated mercy toward him." Jesus told him, "Go and do likewise."

Jesus and the Lawyer

The parable of the good Samaritan, since it is a parable, is a story that Jesus tells. It's not a series of events that actually happened in Jesus's life. Jesus frequently uses parables as a meaningful and memorable way to convey his teachings. Stories stick with us!

Jesus doesn't bring up the story of the good Samaritan out of nowhere, though. He tells it in response to two questions by "a legal expert," or a lawyer, as some other translations say. It's important to understand that being a lawyer in Jesus's times was a different occupation than it is today. Today, lawyers are experts in secular laws put forth by the government. In Jesus's setting, lawyers were mostly experts in religious law, specifically the Jewish system of laws based on the writings attributed to Moses in the Torah. This lawyer, then, is similar to those figures elsewhere called scribes and Pharisees.

The first question the lawyer asks Jesus is "Teacher, what must I do to gain eternal life?" (v. 25). Luke notes that the lawyer asks Jesus this question "to test Jesus." Jesus turns the test around and asks the question back to the lawyer, who responds by quoting Leviticus 19:18, an answer Jesus approves.

The lawyer's question can be a tricky test for us as Protestants too. Protestants emphasize justification by faith. Often, we interpret that to mean that the key to salvation, or eternal life as the lawyer puts it, is our belief. We further interpret "belief" to mean that salvation depends on our mental assent to a series of logical propositions about Jesus, God, the Holy Spirit, and humanity.

The lawyer, though, doesn't ask what he must *believe* to inherit eternal life. He asks what he must *do* to inherit eternal life. Of course, we must assume the lawyer did not have a proper understanding of Christian theology (since there was no such thing at the time). Yet it is significant that Jesus does not correct the question. He doesn't tell the lawyer that he is focusing on the wrong thing by asking about *doing* instead of *believing*.

Wesleyan theology can get us out of this confusion. For John Wesley, salvation is not just about justification (that is, forgiveness of sins and being made right with God) but about sanctification as well. Sanctification is the process of growing in love for God and others. Belief in the sense of mental agreement with a set of propositions is not unimportant for Wesley. But it is just the starting point. Real Christianity for Wesley comes in acting on these beliefs in love. Our active love is not a prerequisite for experiencing God's justifying grace, but it is a necessary result of experiencing God's sanctifying grace. Thus, loving God and loving others is an intrinsic part of Wesley's vision of salvation. Of course, the right answer to the lawyer's question is about active love and not just belief!

If the distinction between believing and doing can cause some confusion, so can the nature of what is meant by "doing" in this passage. When American Christians hear the question, "What must I do?" we often understand that as a question about what list of actions we need to perform. But the answer that the lawyer gives and Jesus affirms makes it clear that "doing" in this sense is about something other than a catalogue of activities. The lawyer's answer is about loving, which is more than just a series of tasks on a to-do list. We would never say, "Well, I've loved the Lord my God with all my heart, being, strength, and mind today. Now that I've got that done, I can go mow the lawn." We understand that loving God is an ongoing process, not a onetime action. Yet we often think of loving others as an item to check off our to-do lists. How many times have you heard someone say, "I've done my good deed for the day"? Loving our neighbors as ourselves, though, is not about doing one good deed per day. It's about an ongoing process of building up a relationship through connections, shared experiences, and mutual trust and affection.

This question and its answer are important to keep in mind in future chapters as we discuss the nature of the good news. Sharing good news is not primarily about conveying a series of truth statements. Nor is it about checking off a list of to-dos as part of a program of helping. It's about modeling and inviting others to a practice of discipleship characterized by active, relational love for God and neighbors.

Befriending, Not Helping

This brings us to the lawyer's second question, "And who is my neighbor?" This is the question that prompts Jesus to tell the story of the good Samaritan. American Christians usually interpret the moral of this question and the parable of the good Samaritan as an answer in the following way: "The good Samaritan loved his neighbor (the traveler) by helping him after he had been beaten up. We should also help other people, which is what Jesus tells us to do so that we can be good people, like the Samaritan." Yet this common understanding of the story misses the mark in several ways.

First, such an interpretation fails to understand what the Samaritan really did with the traveler. Many Christians assume that the Samaritan helped the traveler as a one-time interaction and then went on his way. In doing so, we read our own experiences of transactional interactions into a culture and a situation where something very different was happening. Transactional interactions are interactions that are primarily about doing some sort of business or accomplishing some sort of task and are not part of a longer-term relationship. When we interact with the checkout clerk at the grocery store or visit our doctor or talk to a banker about a loan, these are all transactional interactions. Transactional interactions are short-term and have few implications for future interactions. Perhaps we'll come back to the same grocery store for our next shopping trip, but if we don't, that's not a big deal. Transactional interactions are the norm in modern Western societies, but not in all non-Western societies and certainly not in pre-modern societies, including first-century Palestine.

Most "helping" professions in modern Western societies, including doctors, nurses, social workers, teachers, lawyers, personal care attendants, customer service representatives, and church leaders, are structured around transactional interactions. That's not unique to helping professions; it is generally true of interactions in modern societies that have shifted from relationship-based economies to formalized economies. But because helping professions are included in this switch, we assume that helping involves someone providing a service in a transactional fashion. You might go back to that service provider again for the same or a related service, but you are under no obligation to do so, and the service provider is under no obligation to continue to provide you with services if they decide to move or change jobs.

The good Samaritan, however, is not about helping or providing a service. It's about being a neighbor. The word "neighbor" used in this story implies the start of some sort of long-term relationship, which is the exact opposite of Americans' transactional understanding of service and helping. A "neighbor" means one who is close to you. We usually think of this closeness in a literal and physical sense, but we can also understand that closeness in terms of relationship. Being a neighbor is an ongoing relationship, not a one-off interaction.

In fact, a better term to describe the relationship that develops between the Samaritan and the traveler is perhaps "friend." In the Hebrew version of Leviticus, which the lawyer quotes, the word that's translated as "neighbor" can mean "friend."[1] Our New Testaments use the term "neighbor" because they are based off of the Greek Septuagint text, but Jesus and the lawyer would have been speaking Aramaic, which is closer to Hebrew. Therefore, when Jesus and the lawyer were talking, the term "neighbor" would have meant something broader and much more relational than just "the person who lives next door." It could mean friend, and real friendship requires ongoing relationship. Therefore, the good Samaritan didn't *help* the traveler; he *befriended* the traveler, and he crossed a number of boundaries to do so: ethnic and religious, to name only two. There is a big difference.

When we approach the text thinking of the Samaritan as befriending rather than helping the traveler, we notice some aspects of the story we may have missed before. To start with, the Samaritan and the traveler probably talked on the way to the

---

1 Philologos, "The Bible Says to Love Your Neighbor as Yourself. But What Does Neighbor Mean?" *Mosaic* (Dec. 16, 2015), https://mosaic magazine.com/observation/2015/12/the-bible-says-to-love-your -neighbor-as-yourself-but-what-does-neighbor-mean/, accessed July 24, 2018.

inn. Once you got past Bethany, there wasn't a lot on the road from Jerusalem to Jericho, so it was probably some distance that they had to travel to get to the inn and thus they were traveling for a while. Maybe they just traveled in awkward silence the whole way, and it's probable that the traveler wasn't up for a lot of conversation because of his injuries, but I think it's fair to imagine that the Samaritan and the traveler talked some as they were traveling together. They got to know each other a bit. Whether or not they talked, there was likely some nonverbal communication as well.

When they got to the inn, notice that the Samaritan stayed with the traveler the first night and took care of him. That means that the Samaritan would have stayed in the same room and perhaps even the same bed as the traveler. It was standard for strangers to share a bed in inns, let alone two people who were traveling together, one of them caring for the other. The process of the Samaritan caring for the traveler's wounds that night would have also required physical touch of the traveler's injured body. Physical touch (another boundary) was a sign of relational closeness at the time, as hugs and handshakes still indicate today, even in the West.

When we look for signs of relationship, we also pay more attention when Jesus tells us that the Samaritan planned to come back to the inn after he leaves the traveler there. Certainly, part of the reason the Samaritan came back is to settle any additional charges for the traveler's care, but it would have been awkward for him to come back and not interact with the traveler at all. In all likelihood, the Samaritan came back not just to pay for the traveler's care, but to check on the traveler, to see how he was doing. That is what a friend would do.

Unlikely Friends

Understanding the interaction between the Samaritan and the traveler as befriending rather than helping sets us up to understand the really radical aspect of this story—the way in which their friendship crossed boundaries. The traveler and the Samaritan started out as strangers—there's no reason to think they knew each other prior to this encounter. But even more than strangers, the Samaritan and the traveler started off as potential enemies. Jesus's listeners would have assumed that the traveler in the story was Jewish, like them. Yet Jews and Samaritans were groups with some significant bad blood between them. They had deep-seated religious differences and conflicting claims to the land of Israel. In modern terms, the traveler could be from Israel, and the Samaritan could be a Palestinian. That is what makes the relationship really remarkable. This is a friendship that crosses significant ethnic, religious, and political boundaries all at the same time.

Moreover, this boundary-crossing friendship wasn't just a casual friendship that could be dropped if either the Samaritan or the traveler got too much pressure from their other friends or family for making friends with "the wrong sort" of person. In American culture, there is a gradation of friendships, from Facebook friend to work friend to friends we do certain activities with (golfing buddies, for example) to close friends to best friends. Our level of commitment varies with the type of friendship. We would do almost anything for our best friends, but we would be annoyed if a random Facebook friend showed up unannounced and expected to eat dinner with us.

Yet in Jesus's world (and in many parts of the non-Western world still today), people could expect that level of hospitality from any of their friends. There was no gradation is friendship; all friends were at the "crash on your couch unexpectedly" level of friendship. In Jesus's world, hospitality was an important practice of friendship that reflected some serious obligations and an important connection between the one offering it and the one receiving it. Hospitality could be the difference between life and death. There's a connection between our English words "hospitality" and "hospital." When the Samaritan befriended that traveler, he offered the traveler a form of hospitality in taking care of him physically. But that's exactly what a friend was expected to do for another friend.

Thus, when the Samaritan befriended the traveler, he was letting someone from a feared and shunned group into a close relationship that implied significant mutual obligation between both friends. He wasn't just being kind to a stranger. He was inviting an enemy to become a best friend.

The Samaritan

Once we fully comprehend the radicalness of what the Samaritan was doing, we might be tempted to ask why he befriended the traveler. To answer this question, we'll begin by looking at some of what the story *doesn't* say about the Samaritan.

First, the Samaritan did not befriend the traveler based on preconceived plans for helping others. He wasn't a traveling doctor looking for people to heal. He didn't have a bunch of extra oil, wine, and bandages that he was looking to unload and thought helping the traveler would be a charitable way to use them. He hadn't formed a partnership with the innkeeper to bring any injured people he encountered to the inn. The Samaritan wasn't even on the road from Jerusalem to Jericho looking for opportunities to befriend others across difference. Jesus simply says he "was on a journey." As far as we know, he was just going about his regular business before he encountered the injured traveler.

He was, however, paying attention on his trip. Jesus says that the Samaritan "came to where the man was" and "saw him." Seeing the traveler led the Samaritan to engage with him. The Samaritan befriended the traveler when he noticed him, but he noticed him because he was paying attention. In particular, the Samaritan was willing to pay attention even to someone who was from a very different social and religious group from him. The Samaritan was willing to pay attention across human differences.

When the Samaritan saw the traveler, he felt compassion for him. The New Revised Standard Version says the Samaritan felt "pity," but the Common English Bible says "compassion." Compassion is the better term. In both translations, the lawyer says the neighbor is the "one who demonstrated mercy." Mercy is defined as "compassionate treatment of those in distress."[2] The Samaritan is motivated to help the traveler by compassion. Compassion comes from the Latin for "suffering with." It means feeling another's pain and wanting to do something about it. It is a form of love. This is the difference between the Samaritan on the one hand and the priest and the Levite on the other. Jesus says all three saw the traveler, but only the Samaritan felt compassion. The other two avoided the traveler by crossing to the far side of the road.

> **The Samaritan has compassion on the traveler, because he recognizes a connection between them.**

Compassion and love are based on recognition of shared humanity. The Samaritan has compassion on the traveler, because he recognizes a connection between the two of them. Maybe he thinks, "That could have been me." Certainly, he thinks, "I would want someone to stop for me if I were in that situation." He does NOT think, "I'm so much better than that wounded traveler. I'm going to stop and help him just to prove how good I am." Such focusing on oneself is actually the opposite of compassion, which is about how the other person is feeling, not about how you are feeling. The Samaritan befriended the traveler not to make himself feel good or superior to the traveler, but because he recognized that he would want a friend if he were in that situation.

Because the Samaritan didn't have a preconceived plan of how he should help and because he recognized the traveler as a fellow human in a situation he could have ended up in himself, that left him free to befriend the traveler on the traveler's own

---

2 "Mercy," Merriam-Webster, https://www.merriam-webster.com/dictionary /mercy, accessed July 24, 2018.

terms. In this regard, good news was defined on the traveler's terms, not the Samaritan's. Moreover, good news was determined situationally. After he was beaten up, the best news for the traveler was that there was someone who was willing to befriend him. At other times and places, other forms of good news might have resonated with him but being in that particular situation shaped his perception of good news at that moment.

We can imagine the encounter between the Samaritan and the traveler. The Samaritan probably asked the traveler, "What happened?" to which the traveler would have responded, "I got robbed, and they beat me up." The Samaritan probably next asked, "Where does it hurt?", "Where did they hit you?", and/ or "What can I do?" If the Samaritan did not listen to the traveler and just started to try to treat his injuries without consulting with the traveler, there is actually a chance that he could have caused more harm and made the traveler's injuries worse. Growing up, my Boy Scout first aid training taught that moving injured people without knowing the situation can worsen those injuries. Therefore, you shouldn't start treating someone until you know what's going on with them in the situation at hand, and you can't fully know what's going on with that person in that situation without talking to and listening to the person who has been hurt. Unless the person is completely unconscious, you need to listen to them. We very seldom engage in mission with unconscious people, so we need to listen!

These clarifications about what led the Samaritan to engage in a form of compassionate mission with the traveler should give us pause. Often, especially when North Americans participate in short-term mission trips, whether those are domestic or abroad, we go out looking to help. The danger of such an approach is that when we set out looking to help, we often set out looking for problems to solve. That can reinforce our tendencies to look at others as problems, not as people. As we have seen, though, the Samaritan befriended the traveler exactly *because* he saw the traveler as a fellow human. The recognition of others' common humanity with us is at the foundation of biblical mission.

The Traveler

We can understand this common humanity better when we look not only at the Samaritan but at the traveler as well. It's important to examine the traveler because this Bible passage is often taken to justify what is called a "needs-based" approach to mission. In such an approach, we approach mission by looking at what other people need, what they don't have. This strategy, though, sees other people as "problems" in need of "solutions," which we then provide! It also emphasizes distance and separation between those in mission and those among whom they are in mission, not common humanity. It separates the "haves" of those in mission from the "have-nots" of those among whom they are in mission. This approach overlooks other aspects of the humanity of those on the other side of boundaries—their skills, abilities, knowledge, and other assets. It sees only the positive in those in mission and only the negative in those among whom they are in mission.

Thus, I want to deconstruct this "needs-based" understanding of this passage by looking at exactly what the passage does and does not say about the man who was traveling from Jerusalem to Jericho. This will allow us to go beyond just assuming that he needs help for obvious reasons to ask whether "needing" and "help" are fully adequate ways of thinking about the traveler and his situation.

First, I think it's important to pay attention to what Jesus *doesn't* say about the traveler. This will help us see the traveler in a new light and better understand how the Samaritan ended up befriending him and to what end.

First, Jesus doesn't say, "The traveler fell into the hands of robbers *and* he was poor." In fact, the traveler had to be at least somewhat well-off to have things worth stealing. We are told that the robbers "stripped him," presumably of clothes and other valuables. Nobody steals your smelly ratty old t-shirt, dirty ripped jeans, and $1.47 of pocket change. It's not worth the effort. People steal from those who have something of value. If the traveler had something of value, then he wasn't poor. We can also infer that the Samaritan had at least a moderate amount of money. He owned a donkey or horse and had sufficient currency, which he could spend on the traveler's care at the inn. Nevertheless, he wasn't necessarily rich or even necessarily richer than the traveler. Therefore, this parable is not actually about the rich Samaritan helping the poor traveler, even though we often read it that way.

Second, Jesus doesn't say, "The traveler fell into the hands of robbers *and* he didn't know God." In the minds of Jesus's hearers, the traveler (whom they presumed was Jewish like them) would have known God better than the Samaritan, who was a member of a rival religious group. If Jesus were telling this story to Christians today, it might be the story of the good Muslim instead of the good Samaritan. The fact that the traveler was coming from Jerusalem might even have been a clue that he was particularly religious. If he was on his way home from Jerusalem, he may have been coming from the Temple. The fact that a priest and Levite were going the same way supports this hypothesis. Regardless, the Samaritan was not more religious, and certainly not more Jewish, than the traveler. Therefore, this parable is not about the religious person helping the unreligious person.

Third, Jesus doesn't say, "The traveler fell into the hands of robbers *and* he had no friends and family." The traveler might have had lots of friends and family at home who would gladly have been willing to help him, had he been robbed closer to home. We don't know. The story doesn't say. The story also doesn't say what sort of family and friends the Samaritan had. However, the Samaritan was probably farther away from home than the traveler, so he probably had less of a social network in

Judea than the traveler. Therefore, this parable is not about the well-connected person helping the lonely person.

Jesus *only* says that the traveler had fallen into the hands of robbers, who stripped him, beat him, and left him for dead. By looking at what Jesus *doesn't* say about the traveler, we see that although we tend to focus on the traveler's needs, the traveler was better off in some regards than the Samaritan (religiously, from the per- spective of the Jews, and perhaps in terms of social network), perhaps roughly equal in others (money), and worse off only in this one particular regard—he had been robbed and beaten up.

> Jesus *only* says that the traveler fell into the hands of robbers, who stripped him, beat him, and left him for dead.

In that regard, to the extent that the traveler had needs, they were *situational,* and they were not a reflection of who he was or the entirety of his life. We often mistake situational needs for pervasive needs. We assume that because someone needs help in one particular regard, they need help in all regards. If someone needs help paying their electric bill one month, we assume that must indicate that they also need job training, a grief support group, and/or substance abuse counseling. While it is true that some people experience interconnected challenges in life, if we mistake situational and pervasive needs, we can see others not as persons with a prob- lem but as people with nothing but problems.

Once we mistake situational for pervasive needs, then we often go a step further and infer that those presumed perva- sive needs are a negative reflection on the person experiencing them. In social psychology, there's something called the Fun- damental Misattribution Error—we assume that people behave based on who they are, not the situation they are in. If some- one cuts me off while driving, I assume it's because they're a jerk, not because they're late for work. This, however, may be a misattribution. They may indeed be late for work and a good driver and kind person in general. I think we often make the same mistake regarding the needs we perceive in others. We assume that needs are part of who someone is (or isn't) instead of a reflection of the situation they are in. In so doing, we miss their shared humanity with us.

Being in a particular situation is not a reflection of someone's worth, competence, or abilities, and we need to see past their situation to see the positive aspects of who they are. If you live in a remote mountain town without good cell phone coverage, it's not a sign that you're stupid, lazy, or don't want a cell phone. It's not a sign that you're lonely, poor, or lost. It's just a reflection of the geographic situation you're in and the challenges of providing cell service *in that situation*. You may even have knowledge and skills that could help bring better cell service to your town. If others assume that you're stupid, lazy, poor, or uninterested, they may overlook those useful knowledge sets and skills. Similarly, if you live in a remote rural village in Cambodia with limited medical facilities, it's not a sign that you're stupid, lazy, or don't want good medical care. It's not a sign that you're lonely, poor, or lost. It's just a reflection of the situation you're in and the challenges of providing medical care *in that situation*. You may even have knowledge and skills that could help bring better medical care to your town. If others assume that you're stupid, lazy, poor, or uninterested, they may overlook those useful knowledge sets and skills.

> **When we engage in mission, we cannot assume that others are all needs.**

Thus, we must warn ourselves, when we are reading the good Samaritan and when we are engaged in mission, not to assume that others are all needs. We must not overlook the assets they possess because they also have some needs. And we must not assume that any of their needs make them fundamentally different from us. The Samaritan didn't do any of these things, and neither should we.

Are We the Traveler?

Usually, when most Christians read this story, we assume that we are the Samaritan in this story. After all, the Samaritan is the "good" character, and we want to be good, too! Yet, if we pay close attention to the conclusion of the conversation between Jesus and the lawyer, we see that this may not be what Jesus intends.

Remember, the story is a response to the question, "Who is my neighbor?" or in other words, "Who should I love?" After telling the parable, Jesus asks the lawyer who the neighbor was. The lawyer responds, "The one who showed mercy." The neighbor is the Samaritan. Jesus is saying his hearers should love the Samaritan. If the Samaritan is the one we should love, then we are not the Samaritan.

If we are not the Samaritan, we might be the traveler in the story. We should love those who befriend us and show mercy to us, even when they are different from us and are our potential enemies. Anglican theologian Samuel Wells not only argues for this "minority reading" of the parable of the good Samaritan, he notes that Charles Wesley took this interpretation in his hymn "Woe is me! What tongue can tell."[3] Wells argues that part of identifying with the traveler in the ditch means that we need to admit to our own hurts, needs, and shortcomings. His book is addressed primarily to Westerners, whose relative affluence allows them to ignore the ways in which they are broken. Yet the parable is, in Wells's reading of it, a challenge for us to admit to our own brokenness, for it is only by doing so that we can

---

3   See chapter 6 of Samuel Wells, *A Nazareth Manifesto: Being with God* (Malden, MA: Wiley Blackwell, 2015). The term "minority reading" and reference to Charles Wesley are in fn. 4 on p. 98.

experience the good news of God's love and healing, which often comes to us in the form of people we despise.

Jesus does say to the lawyer at the end of the parable, "Go and do likewise." This is clearly a call to show mercy and have compassion as the Samaritan did. Yet it is possible to understand this instruction not as an order to be the Samaritan in the story, but as a challenge to love the Samaritan back when we are the traveler. Understood that way, Jesus's instruction is a challenge to the lawyer to be willing to reciprocate when he experiences compassion from those he considers different from himself. That reciprocity can mean a willingness to gratefully receive from those who are different from and even repulsive to us. Or it can mean a willingness to accept our obligations of friendship when we are befriended by those who are different from and repulsive to us. Or it can mean both.

When we engage in mission with others, there will be many times when we receive hospitality, mercy, and compassion from those among whom we are in mission. That can vary from the literal hospitality that is involved in being hosted on a mission trip, to offers of prayer for us, to gifts given to us by those we think we are serving. When we experience such compassion from others, are we willing to be vulnerable about our brokenness, receive their compassion, let ourselves be befriended, and commit to an ongoing relationship with our mission partners?

The Rest of the Story

Whether we see ourselves as the Samaritan or the traveler in the story or even another character, it is worthwhile to think about the result of the Samaritan befriending the traveler. To start with, that result was not for the Samaritan to continue to help the traveler forever, nor was it to create dependence by the traveler on the Samaritan. People heal from their wounds. Therefore, we can reasonably expect the traveler to have healed from his wounds. Indeed, the people in the story seem to expect the traveler to heal from his wounds. The exchange between the Samaritan and the innkeeper presumes that the traveler will get better and will only need a finite amount of care.

Thus, the Samaritan wasn't undertaking to pay all of the traveler's medical expenses for the rest of his life. Eventually, probably within a few weeks if not a few days, the traveler was able to take care of himself again. Nor was the Samaritan setting up an employment program for the traveler or pairing the traveler with a foster family or trying to connect him to a church. Remember, the traveler didn't need any of these things. He wasn't poor, there's no indication he was lonely, and he was already religious. The traveler's need was situational. Once that situation was addressed, there was no need for the Samaritan to keep helping the traveler.

In fact, the Samaritan could only have continued to help the traveler with wounds from being beaten up if he had continued to beat him up! Since the Samaritan had compassion on the traveler and befriended him, we can assume he did not do that. If the Samaritan had continued to beat up the traveler, he would have been a terrible friend!

Sometimes mission partners among the poor of the world do see well-to-do Christians as bad friends because of their support for economic and political systems that continually "beat up" the poor. Just as the traveler would have wanted the Samaritan to listen if he had said, "You're standing on my foot!" we must also be willing to listen when our mission partners express their pains from the unjust structures of the world. Moreover, we must be willing to reconsider our place in these structures, just as we would hope the Samaritan would have reconsidered where he was standing.

Friendship is give and take.

It is possible that the Samaritan helped the traveler with other situations in the future, since that possibility is within the scope of friendship, but it is just as likely that the traveler helped the Samaritan with other situations in the future. While friends might help each other from time to time, friendship is not about one person always helping the other person. It's about give and take.

In the future, the traveler could just as easily have helped the Samaritan if he needed help. Relationship allows both parties to experience the good news of God's love and each other's love. And perhaps together, the traveler and the Samaritan were able to share more good news with others.

So, the traveler and the Samaritan became friends and neighbors, and that was an ongoing relationship. Relationship is the result of living like Jesus instructs us to. While care for his injuries was good news for the traveler while he was lying on the side of the road, in the long-term, this relationship across extreme differences with the Samaritan was even better news.

■ MISSION TAKEAWAYS

What can we take from this parable that's relevant to how we think about mission? What can it teach us about how to do mission and what the goals of mission are? We can identify three takeaways:

1. Make friendship the goal of mission, not helping. Just as the Samaritan didn't help the traveler forever, don't seek to keep helping your mission partners forever. Certainly, don't hurt others so that you can keep helping them! Instead of a helper/helpee relationship, seek to develop a friend/friend relationship based on compassion and common humanity, even across bitter human boundaries, just as the Samaritan and the traveler did.

2. As you are developing relationships, assume there is more to people than whatever situations they may be in, just like there was more to the traveler than being robbed. Assume people's needs are situational, not a reflection of them as a person. Recognize their assets. Listen to people's own understanding of their situations, just like the Samaritan listened to and responded to the traveler's situation. Don't come in with preconceived plans of what you want to do for them.

3. As part of the process of relationship formation, be open
    to being helped by those with whom you are in mission,
    even when they come from despised groups. Be vulner-
    able about your own hurts and weaknesses. Be willing to
    receive from them. When you do so, you demonstrate
    your recognition of their common humanity and your rec-
    ognition of the assets that they have.

■ DISCUSSION QUESTIONS

Use these questions to guide group study of this chapter or for
individual reflection:

1. Think about a close friendship in your life. In what ways
    has that friendship been "good news" to you? In what
    ways has it been "good news" to your friend?
2. What kinds of assumptions do we sometimes make about
    the people we reach out to in mission?
3. What kinds of assumptions might people make about
    your church? What kind of first impressions do people
    have of your church? Are they true?
4. Think about a problem in your life. What would you not
    want others to assume about you based on that problem?
    Have you ever had others make assumptions about you?
5. Think of a time when someone did not listen to you when
    you tried to explain something to them. How did this feel?
    How did you respond?
6. Think about a mission project or mission trip you or your
    church participated in. What was the goal of the mission
    project or mission trip? Who defined that goal? What role
    did those with whom you were in mission have in defining
    that goal? What were the results of the mission trip?
7. Think about a form of mission you or your church is cur-
    rently engaged in. What assets do you have? What assets
    do they have? How are their assets relevant to the work

you do with them? What can they give in addition to (or instead of) whatever they may receive from you?

8. What would it look like for you as an individual or as a church group to be vulnerable in your mission relationships? How would you approach being honest about your own brokenness?

9. Think about a mission project or mission trip you or your church participated in. Were there long-term relationships that came out of that mission project or mission trip (i.e., relationships that extended beyond just the duration of the project or trip)? If so, who were the relationships with? Were they with other people in mission, or were they with your mission partners? What were these relationships like? If no long-term relationships came out of that mission project or mission trip, why didn't any arise?

■ FURTHER READING

Here are some other books related to topics in this chapter and why you should read them:

Greg Barrett, *The Gospel of Rutba: War, Peace, and the Good Samaritan Story in Iraq* (Maryknoll, NY: Orbis Books, 2012). This story from the early days of the Iraq War reverses the roles we expect in the good Samaritan story: here, Western Christian peacemakers are the (literally) injured travelers and Iraqi Muslims are the good Samaritans who befriend the injured travelers despite human boundaries of war and enmity. The story highlights the relationships and the peacemaking collaboration that comes out of this good Samaritan encounter.

David I. Smith, *Learning from the Stranger: Christian Faith and Cultural Diversity* (Grand Rapids, MI: William B. Eerdmans Publishing Company, 2009). Smith argues that Christians in mission, especially Western, white Christians, must be prepared to learn culturally and linguistically from those different from them, not just seek to impart their understanding to others. Smith draws on the parable of the good Samaritan in his theology, seeing Western Christians in the role of the injured traveler needing to receive from the Samaritan.

E. Randolph Richards and Brandon J. O'Brien, *Misreading Scripture with Western Eyes: Removing Cultural Blinders to Better Understand the Bible* (Downers Grove, IL: IVP Books, 2012). This chapter argues that we often misunderstand scripture (such as the parable of the good Samaritan, though it is not directly addressed in Richards and O'Brien's book) because of the cultural assumptions we bring to it, and that such misunderstandings can have serious implications for how we go about mission. Richards and O'Brien do an excellent job of unpacking how Western culture includes assumptions that cause us to commit just such misreadings, which can complicate our relationships with Christians from other cultures.

Philip Jenkins, *The New Faces of Christianity: Believing the Bible in the Global South* (New York: Oxford University Press, 2006). Philip Jenkins's examination of Christianity in Africa and Asia highlights how important the Bible is for Christians in these lands and the sometimes surprising (to Westerners) ways in which they interpret the Bible through the cultural and theological perspectives they bring to the Bible. The book provides an interesting complement to Richards and O'Brien's book above.

Heard Any Good News Lately?

3

*"The beginning of the good news about
Jesus Christ, God's Son." (Mark 1:1)*

An Abundance of Good News

Good news is at the heart of Christianity and at the heart of Christian mission. Mark identifies his account of the life, ministry, death, and resurrection of Jesus as "the good news about Jesus Christ, God's Son." Indeed, the term "gospel," the name usually given to the biblical books written by Matthew, Mark, Luke, and John, literally means "good news." Christians believe that the story of Jesus is good news! For early Christians, this concept was central to how they understood what it meant to be a Christian. Throughout the Acts of the Apostles, there are numerous references to Christians preaching "the good news," and the apostle Paul refers to himself as one who has been "set apart for God's good news" (Romans 1:1).

> **Good news is at the heart of Christianity and at the heart of Christian mission.**

In chapter 1, we discussed how mission begins with God (what missiologists refer to as the *missio Dei*, the mission of God) and God's love for the world. The message of God's love for the world is conveyed by God sending Jesus, God and Jesus sending the Holy Spirit, and Jesus sending his disciples. Mission is grounded in this message of love that God sends to the world. And this message is not bad news to the world; God is sending good news! We should treat it as such and present it with joy.[1]

Mission thus is centrally about the good news, which is basic to Christianity. Without it, not only would there be no mission; there would be no Christianity. Being a Christian is about claiming the story of God's good news as the story of our lives as well. It's about finding our place in the conversation of the saints of all times and places. And it's about the God who loves us and who, because of that love, came down to earth in the person of Jesus to set us free, heal our wounds, forgive our sins, renew the world in which we live, and restore our relationships.

> There is no such thing as a solitary Christian.

Methodism has always been clear that while being a Christian involves finding our place in the story of God's good news, that place is never a solitary one. When we become Christians, when we recognize and respond to God's gracious love, we are connected to other Christians. We become part of the ongoing conversation of the Christian faith, a conversation in which Christians throughout the world and throughout the ages share their understanding of God's good news.

Furthermore, when we experience the good news of God's love, we are compelled to share God's love with everyone, Christian or not. When we truly experience the good news of God's

---

1   Appropriately, Dana L. Robert's United Methodist Women study of mission is entitled *Joy to the World! Mission in the Age of Global Christianity* (New York: Women's Division, General Board of Global Ministries, The United Methodist Church, 2010).

love, we want to talk with others about it! We want to know if they, too, have experienced this love, to learn from them if they have, and to encourage them to look for it if they haven't. Moreover, we want to demonstrate God's love for others in our actions as well as our conversations. In short, when we truly experience God's love, we want to engage in mission. Good news is thus both the message of, and the motivation for, mission.

Yet just what is this good news about which God wants us to engage the world in mission? As good Christians, we may think we know, but the answer to that question may not be as simple as it seems. The gospel writers don't precisely clarify what they mean by "good news." This chapter will look at four different senses in which the terms "good news" and "gospel" are used in the New Testament: as the Kingdom of God, as freedom from sin, as resurrection, and as restoration of relationship.

There's a Wideness

In addition to gaining a better understanding of the biblical meaning of "good news," this survey of these different aspects of good news gets at another point, one that is critical to the rest of the book: people can legitimately and faithfully understand God's good news in multiple ways. In the conversation among Christians of all places and ages, faithful people have had differ- ent takes on how best to understand God's good news. Even the Bible speaks about good news in a variety of ways. Not only are there four different biblical forms of good news in this chapter, it is also possible to interpret each of these four in varying, but legitimate, ways.

This insight is consistent with our belief in a God who sur- passes human understanding. Just as God is beyond our ability to fully comprehend, so too is God's good news. We shouldn't limit God's good news to just one thing; when we do, we con- strain God's power and love to just one aspect. God is bigger than that. Seeking the breadth of God's good news recognizes the scope of God's amazing love and amazing power. It releases us from the boxes into which we try to put God and confronts us with the awe-inspiring vastness of God's love for God's creation. God's good news isn't a single story or even a single newspaper. It's a whole subscription! Our love for God should make us want to know more about God's love for us.

This makes sense with our everyday experience. To say one thing is good news doesn't mean something else isn't also good news. If my brother gets a new job and my aunt is healed from disease, those are both pieces of good news. One doesn't negate the other. To say that because the forgiveness of sin is good news, the establishment of God's kingdom isn't, or to say that because the restoration of relationship is good news, resurrection isn't, is not just bad theology; it's a bad understanding of how good news works in general!

While we often have theological debates about the precise definition of good news, that is the wrong approach. There is value in theological clarity, but clarity is not the same as narrowness. Instead of seeking a limited definition, we should seek the wideness and fullness of God's good news. Thus, God's good news involves both personal forgiveness and social change. God's good news involves both body and spirit. God's good news involves both heaven and earth. God's good news is not a needle point, honed and sharp. It's a panorama, providing an expansive view of beauty.

If God's good news is wide and not narrow, then we must also admit something else: we don't know it all. We may be sent as messengers of God's good news, but we ourselves do not know the full message. Therefore, it is only through conversation with others that we discover more of the fullness and wideness of God's good news. Others will have their own sense of what's good about God's good news and what's new about it. We must share our understanding with them, but we must also be willing to listen to their understandings. Chapters 5 and 6 will explore this process in greater detail. But first, we turn to the Bible.

The Good News of the Kingdom

The Synoptic Gospels (Matthew, Mark, and Luke) agree that Jesus's good news is related to the kingdom of God/heaven. (Matthew prefers the term "kingdom of heaven" instead of Mark's and Luke's "kingdom of God," perhaps because of Matthew's Jewish sensitivities about using the name of God.) In Matthew's description of Jesus's ministry, he writes that Jesus "announced the good news of the kingdom and healed every disease and sickness among the people" (Matthew 4:23; see also Matthew 9:35). Similarly, Mark describes the start of Jesus's ministry in this way: "Jesus came into Galilee announcing God's good news, saying, 'Now is the time! Here comes God's kingdom! Change your hearts and lives, and trust this good news!'" (Mark 1:14-15). Luke, too, refers to Jesus "preaching and proclaiming the good news of God's kingdom" (Luke 8:1).

What is this kingdom of God that was so closely tied to the good news brought by Jesus? First and foremost, it involves committing our allegiance to and recognizing our dependence upon God in the person of Jesus. In Acts 10:36, Peter says that "the good news through Jesus Christ" is that God "is Lord of all!" Paul identifies as good news not only the news that Jesus is God's Son, but that he is "our Lord" (Romans 1:2-4). We are called to be citizens of the kingdom of heaven, wherein our ultimate loyalty is to Jesus as our Lord. Acknowledging Jesus as Lord means setting aside all other things that clamor for our highest loyalty in life, whether that be country, economic system, race, family, tribe, or any other human construct. Moreover, in the Old English, the word "lord" meant not just ruler but one who gives bread. When we recognize Jesus as Lord, we are not only submitting ourselves to Jesus's will, we are also recognizing that he is the bread of life that feeds us and fills us. Again, we recognize that if Jesus is Lord and the source of our deepest satisfaction, then other things—our wealth, status, goods, reputation, and the pleasures of life—are not.

Although it may reject the claims of the kingdoms of this world to ultimate authority, the kingdom of God is not like worldly political kingdoms. It is not about substituting one human authority structure for another. Many of Jesus's contemporaries misunderstood him on this point. They expected him to claim political power and throw the Roman Empire out of the land of Israel, but Jesus made it clear that was not the type of kingdom he was preaching about.

Instead, the kingdom of God seems to be connected to God's intention to lovingly care for humanity, especially those considered the lowest and the least. Howard Thurman referred to such people as "those who stand . . . with their backs against the wall."[2] While worldly kingdoms focus on the rich and powerful, God's kingdom focuses instead on the poor and marginalized. While worldly kingdoms are about dominance over the poor and weak, God's kingdom is about humble, loving service to exactly such people.

In Luke 4, Jesus makes it clear that the poor and marginalized are the focus of his ministry. In the public launch of his ministry, he reads Isaiah 61 as a description of that ministry:

> The Spirit of the Lord is upon me,
>   because the Lord has anointed me.
> He has sent me to preach good news to the poor,
>   to proclaim release to the prisoners
>   and recovery of sight to the blind,
>   to liberate the oppressed,
>   and to proclaim the year of the Lord's favor
> (Luke 4:18-19).

In quoting Isaiah in this way, Jesus identifies his good news about the kingdom as also being "good news to the poor." Release would also be experienced as good news by prisoners, recovery

---

2   Howard Thurman, *Jesus and the Disinherited* (Boston: Beacon Press, 1996), 11.

of sight would be good news to the blind, and liberation would be good news to the oppressed. The poor, prisoners, the blind, and the oppressed were all among the lowest and the least in Jesus's society, but Jesus fulfills and embodies God's love for exactly these people. His ministry is an expression of God's favor to these marginalized people.

While the kingdom of God is not a worldly kingdom, it does seem to involve God caring for people in the midst of their very worldly problems. That is evident in the ministry overview above from Luke. Poverty, imprisonment, and oppression are all worldly afflictions, not just metaphors for spiritual maladies. We have also seen the connection between good news and worldly problems already in Matthew. Matthew mentions in the same breath Jesus announcing the good news of the kingdom and his healing disease and sickness. The gospels agree that healing people from their illnesses and casting out demons is an important part of Jesus's ministry on earth. Certainly, in a world with lots of endemic disease and no health-care system, healing from disease was very good news! Whether you see the demons Jesus cast out as representatives of spiritual, psychological, or physical maladies, being freed from such sources of suffering would have been good news too.

Concern with the poor, marginalized, sick, and suffering is also tied to the kingdom of God in Jesus's interaction with John the Baptist's disciples recounted in Matthew 11 and Luke 7. When John's disciples ask Jesus if he is "the one who is to come," that is, the Messiah, Jesus responds, "Those who were blind are able to see. Those who were crippled are walking. People with skin diseases are cleansed. Those who were deaf now hear. Those who were dead are raised up. The poor have good news proclaimed to them" (Matthew 11:5). Here Jesus is again echoing Isaiah, both chapters 61 and 35. In this response, Jesus identifies the audience for his good news as the poor. Moreover, he uses preaching to the poor and his healing ministry as proof that he is indeed sent from God as the Messiah. In other words, John's disciples can trust that Jesus is acting out a central role in God's mission to the world because of his concern for the poor and the healing he provides to the suffering.

Not all readers of this book may have had the experience of being monetarily poor, though some will. Yet all of us have had the experience of sickness and suffering. We know what it is to be in pain and to long for reprieve. We can think of instances in our lives in which we experienced the good news of healing, relief of suffering, and an improvement in our fortunes. We may think of that time when the cancer went into remission, when we finally got a job after months of fruitless applications, when we were able to put the demons of drinking and drug use behind us, when we found a community that loved us for who we are in the midst of a world that proclaimed that "our kind" wasn't welcome or worthy. These are instances of the good news of the kingdom!

If Jesus's concern for the poor and for healing the suffering of others is evidence that he is a central part of God's mission, then Christians in mission, who seek to represent God in Christ not only through our words but through our actions, should also show concern for the poor, the marginalized, the sick, and the suffering. Jesus saw this as a key component of his good news, and so should we.

There are many ways in which we can engage in this type of mission. Poverty relief, social justice advocacy, disaster relief, economic development, education, social services, medical care, mental health services, charismatic healing, and more can all be expressions of the good news of the kingdom of God. Such mission with the poor must begin with an affirmation of the value in God's eyes of those who are poor and suffer. When we begin with this affirmation, it sets us on the path of a right missional partnership with the poor and suffering. It allows us to be motivated by compassion and identification with the poor and not by pity, as in the story of the good Samaritan.

When we recognize the importance of the poor in God's eyes, we will seek not to help them from our sense of superiority, but to cultivate their assets, to listen to their perceptions of their situation, and to try to grasp their perspectives on what would constitute good news to them. God may know beforehand what would be "good news to the poor," but since we are not God, we need to be in conversation with the poor and suffering about what they see as good news. If we listen carefully, we can work with them to help bring about that good news and even receive some good news ourselves in the process. This sharing of good news to the poor can become a mutual one. When we approach the financially poor as equals, we can become better prepared to recognize the forms of poverty in our own lives—spiritual, social, relational, etc.—and hear God's good news to us in the midst of our own poverty.

The Good News of Freedom from Sin

Another important dimension of good news in the New Testament is freedom from sin. In Peter's summary of the "good news" in Acts 10, he concludes by saying, "All the prophets testify about [Jesus] that everyone who believes in him receives forgiveness of sins through his name" (v. 43). In Paul's synopsis of the "good news" he preaches, given in 1 Corinthians 15, he starts by saying, "Christ died for our sins in line with the scriptures, he was buried, and he rose on the third day in line with the scriptures" (v. 3-4). This theme occurs elsewhere throughout the epistles.

"Sin" is a complex (and often unpopular) word. Many theological volumes have been written about its exact nature. It can apply both to acts and a state of being. Those actions can range from intentionally breaking laws to making mistakes. That state of being has been thought of as guilt, as evil, or as being in conflict. I cannot delve into a complete examination of the full range of meanings of the word "sin" here. Nevertheless, it is important to acknowledge that "freedom from sin" is a complex topic that can be understood in many different ways. This is another reminder that to truly understand what's good about God's good news, we need to be in conversation, so as to learn from others who are different than us, even on topics we may think we know so well as the forgiveness of sin.

I do, however, want to highlight one difference in understanding sin and its forgiveness. This one example will give some sense of the theological variety out there. It is also an example that is central to Wesleyan theology. Furthermore, it is a clear example of how learning from others' understanding of sin can help us increase our own understanding of God's good news.

Western Christians (including both Catholics and Protestants) have often thought about sin in judicial terms such as law, guilt, punishment, etc. In this sense, sin is seen both as individual violations of the law and as the state of guiltiness that comes from such violations. Such violations require a penalty or punishment. Freedom from sins then means canceling the punishment due from law-breaking deeds and removing us from our state of guiltiness. Western Christians have understood the mechanics of this process in various ways, but the basic perspective on sin in Western Europe has been a legal one.

But this legal framework is not the only way to think about sin and forgiveness. Eastern Christians (that is, Eastern Orthodox) have instead often used organic and physical terms to describe sin. In this account, sin is a disease that infects one's being and corrupts one's nature and predisposes us toward evil. Sin is the presence of greed, lust, violent anger, and other dispositions in our soul that run counter to God's nature. Sin is less about individual bad acts that produce a state of guiltiness and more about a corrupted nature that produces individual bad actions. Freedom from sin, then, is less about commuting punishment for individual offenses and more about being healed from our diseased ways of behaving and being so that we can produce good fruit instead of bad fruit.

John Wesley, the founder of the Methodist movement, grew up in a Western tradition that emphasized a legal understanding of sin. But he was also a well-read scholar who sought to understand Eastern Christian perspectives on sin. It was the bringing together of these two perspectives—Western and Eastern—that led Wesley to his full understanding of sin, which incorporated both perspectives. According to Wesley, sin was both guilt that was done away with through the process of justification *and* a disease affecting one's soul that was healed through the process of sanctification. In justification, we are declared "not guilty" before God. Through sanctification, humans are healed of the sickness of sin and restored to the full image of God in which they were created.

We can see this dual understanding of sin and freedom from it in some of the hymns John's brother Charles Wesley penned. In verse 4 of "O For a Thousand Tongues to Sing," Charles writes, "[Jesus] breaks the power of canceled sin."[3] According to Wesleyan theology, sin has already been "canceled" for Christians, in that the guilt of sin has been removed through justification. Yet it is still necessary for Jesus to "break the power" that sin still has over our habits, our minds, and our hearts, even after this removal of guilt. It is still necessary for our natures to be healed of the disease of sin. The breaking of that power of sin occurs through the ongoing work of the Holy Spirit in sanctification.

The Wesleys were willing to learn from others different from them about how they understood God's good news, and this willingness to learn gave Methodism one of its central and most distinctive doctrines. Moreover, the Wesleys realized that there could be value in not necessarily choosing one phrasing of good news over the other but from combining different views. In this regard, the Wesleys' approach to reconciling Western and Eastern frameworks for understanding sin can be a model for us in mission.

In whatever way it is understood, contemporary Americans may struggle with the term "sin." We do not like to be told by

---

3   Charles Wesley, "O For a Thousand Tongues to Sing," 1739. *The United Methodist Hymnal* (Nashville: The United Methodist Publishing House, 1989), 57.

others what we should or should not be doing, nor do we like having our motivations or character questioned. Yet even Americans, like the rest of the world, have experiences of the good news of forgiveness for our wrongs and freedom from our temptations. American or not, we can think of times when we know we hurt someone, but they chose to forgive us instead of holding a grudge. We can think of times when we were able to resist the temptations we experience—whether those are the temptation to lose our tempers with our children, to eat that extra donut, to visit that pornographic website, to tell that gossipy story, or others. Resisting once is usually not the end of the story of temptation, but we experience as good news each time when we act more like the people we want to be and more like the people God wants us to be. Moreover, as Methodists we believe that such good news comes about not just through our own moral exertions, but through the assistance of the Holy Spirit working within us. That can be another important form of good news: we're not just left to rely on our own fallible willpower in our struggles to be and do better. God is with us.

If forgiveness, the ability to be a better person, and the knowledge that we don't have to do so on our own are good news, then they are worth sharing. Evangelism, social work, counseling, education, and others can all be means by which to share this type of good news. While talking about sin may seem like bad news, remember that the good news isn't the sin—it's the freedom from it! Whether or not they use the term "sin," most people struggle with regrets, with unfulfilled aspirations for how they live their lives, with a sense of alienation from God and others, and/or with shame for their inability to live up to their ideals. The bad news already exists in others' lives and in our own, whatever terms they or we use for it. Mission occurs when we enter into dialogue with others to identify or clarify the good news that is present in the midst of this bad news—for them and for us!

The Good News of Resurrection

A third dimension of good news in the New Testament is resurrection. In its most basic sense, resurrection refers to Jesus's resurrection from the dead and its significance as an assurance of our own resurrection after death. When Paul preached to the synagogue at Antioch, he connected the good news and Jesus's resurrection. He stated, "We proclaim to you the good news. What God promised to our ancestors, he has fulfilled for us, their children, by raising up Jesus" (Acts 13:32-33). For Paul, Jesus's resurrection is the central piece of evidence that Jesus is indeed the Son of God, and thus the message of Jesus is a credible one. Because it demonstrates God's love for us and proves Jesus's nature as God, God raising up Jesus is good news!

God raising up Jesus is not only good news in its own right, but it also points to the broader good news it foreshadows. When Paul summarizes his good news at the beginning of 1 Corinthians 15, it's for the sake of setting up an extended argument, making the case that God will resurrect the dead, and using Jesus's own resurrection as the key piece of evidence. Paul concludes his argument by quoting Isaiah in saying, "Death has been swallowed up by a victory," (v. 54b) and then exclaiming, "Thanks be to God, who gives us this victory through our Lord Jesus Christ!" (v. 57). Or, as 2 Timothy 1:10 says, "Now [God's] grace is revealed through the appearance of our savior, Christ Jesus. He destroyed death and brought life and immortality into clear focus through the good news." We will triumph over death because Jesus did. Our resurrection is clearly good news for Paul, and I suspect for many others the idea that life does not end with death is good news as well.

Resurrection after death is, by definition, not something that we can experience in this life. We will have to wait to find out the exact nature of that part of God's good news. Yet resurrection can entail more than just the experience of resurrection after death. Resurrection also implies hope that life will overcome death. We do not have to wait to experience that hope. As Paul writes in

Colossians 1:5-6a, "You have this faith and love because of the hope reserved for you in heaven. You previously heard about this hope through the true message, the good news, which has come to you." In one sense, the hope Paul writes of is "in heaven"; yet it is also part of the faith and love that the Colossian Christians experience in their everyday lives. Hope is a current experience of trust in a future event. Moreover, Paul directly connects this hope with good news. The good news of resurrection is that, in Jesus, God is overcoming death with life in this world and the next, and we may have hope in that.

While none of us has (yet) experienced resurrection from the dead, everyone alive has experience with hope. We know that hope can be very good news, especially when it comes after a period of hopelessness. Throughout this chapter, I have invited you to recall instances of good news in your own lives. Now think back to the time just before you got that good news. Sometimes we are completely surprised by good news and have no idea it is coming. Other times, good news comes as a fulfillment of our hopes. That process of hoping is not the same thing as having the thing hoped for, but it prepares us to meet with joy what we have longed for when it does come. It is a foretaste, an anticipation. And it is a source of strength and perseverance—something that keeps us going, even in the face of tragedy and suffering. Hope is an expression of life.

Moreover, while no one alive has experienced life after death, we can all recognize instances of life triumphing over death in this present life. Whether that comes in the form of healing from physical disease, healing from suicidal thoughts, comfort and connection after the loss of a loved one, or choosing to embrace the good aspects of life instead of focusing on the bad, we can all think of instances of the good news of life triumphing over death—of everyday resurrections.

While evangelism is the form of mission that deals most directly with the hope of resurrection from physical death into eternal life, ideally all mission that we carry out is a form of hope and everyday resurrection. It expresses our faith in a God who promises abundant life and our hope for a world that is more alive and living better than the world we see around us. It expresses our hope that the world can be less violent, less unjust, involve less suffering. It expresses our hope that there can be more love and less hate. It expresses our hope for the well-being of the life of our planet and the plants and animals with whom we share it. It expresses our hope that we ourselves can be better, more loving, and more like Jesus.

Yet hope is not a Christian monopoly. Instead, it seems to be part of the prevenient grace God has given to all—an ability to imagine, to sense, to long for a better world and better selves. We should engage in our mission with a sense of hope but also a willingness to listen to the hopes of others, the ways in which they would like to see life overcome death. Along with that willingness to listen to their hopes, we must risk being vulnerable in sharing where we ourselves have experienced death and despair in our lives and what hopes we hold for ourselves in such situations. Then we must watch and work together with them and with the Holy Spirit to see how God will bring such hopes for resurrection to pass, for them and for us.

The Good News of Restored Relationship

Yet another way to understand good news is as restored relationship. This version of good news is directly connected to (though distinct from) the good news of freedom from sin. While relationships can be understood apart from the concept of sin (as the number of secular relationship self-help books show), I think using the concept of sin to help us understand the restoration of relationship provides a properly theological approach to this topic.

Sin involves both injury to others and shame in oneself for one's misdeeds. In this way, sin destroys relationships. It separates us from God and from others. Injury can happen through direct personal action but also through our inaction and through our participation in harmful systems, even when we do not intend to harm others. Moreover, injury can happen even when we are unaware of the harm we have caused others, either directly or indirectly. Whatever the nature of the injury, when we injure others, we push them away, causing them to withdraw from us for the sake of their own well-being. We alienate others through our sin.

Shame, on the other hand, causes us to withdraw from others, whether or not the other person feels injured. For those from non-Western cultures, this link between shame and damaged relationships will seem self-evident. Yet even within the West, the recent work of social worker Brené Brown has highlighted the extent to which shame can make us withdraw from others.[4] When we feel shame, we want to hide from others, lest they see our shame and look down on us. This desire to hide applies not just to other humans but to God. In that archetypical example, Adam and Eve hid themselves from God after their sin because they were ashamed (Genesis 3:1-13). Moreover, shame can even cause us to hide from ourselves when we are unwilling to admit our mistakes. Sin alienates us from others, God, and ourselves.

If sin involves injury to others and shame in ourselves, then forgiveness of sin heals those injuries and frees us from shame. It undoes that process of alienation. In the process, it restores relationships—with others, God, and ourselves—and allows them to flourish. That restoration of relationship is another central aspect of good news in the New Testament, and relational language to describe good news is found throughout the New Testament writings.

In his description of good news in Colossians 1, Paul writes, "Once you were alienated from God and you were enemies with

---

4   Brené Brown, *The Gifts of Imperfection: Let Go of Who You Think You're Supposed to Be and Embrace Who You Are* (Center City, MN: Hazelden Publishing, 2010).

him in your minds, which was shown by your evil actions. But now he has reconciled you by his physical body through death, to present you before God as a people who are holy, faultless, and without blame" (v. 21-22). The terms Paul uses here—alienated vs. reconciled—are relational terms. Alienation implies the lack of or loss of relationship; reconciliation is healing or restoring a damaged relationship. The good news Paul shares is that our relationship with God, which was damaged, can be restored, and we can once more be in relationship with God.

Nor are these the only relational terms that Paul uses throughout his letters. Paul also speaks about our becoming God's people (2 Corinthians 6:16; see also 1 Peter 2), our adoption as God's children (Romans 8), and our becoming heirs of God (Romans 8:17, Galatians 3:25-4:7). All three of these important images for Paul speak directly to our relationship with God. The first of these images, of being God's people, may also have connotations of the good news of the kingdom. The image of Christians as the body of Christ is also very important to Paul (Romans 12; 1 Corinthians 12; Colossians 1), and it's hard to image a more direct and relational connection than being part of the same body. Moreover, the terms redemption, atonement, and reconciliation should also be understood in very relational ways. While Western Christians often think of these words in legal terms, they are all processes that are intended to restore right relationship. To focus on the legal technicalities of the process is to risk missing the relational nature of the goal. What this plethora of relationship terms and metaphors used by Paul indicates is that the restoration of relationship, however expressed, is central to understanding the nature of God's good news.

The good news about restored relationships does not stop with our relationships with God, either. In 1 Peter 1, Peter instructs Christians, "As you set yourselves apart by your obedience to the truth so that you might have genuine affection for your fellow believers, love each other deeply and earnestly" (v. 22). Peter explains that Christians will do this because they are reborn from "the word that was proclaimed to you as good news" (v. 23, 25). Restored relationships with other humans characterized by deep and earnest love are both a response to hearing good news and a form of good news itself!

John Wesley identified four types of relationships that are restored through the good news of Christianity: our relationship with God, our relationship with other humans, our relationship with animals and the rest of creation, and our relationship with ourselves.[5] Following his understanding of freedom from sin as healing our diseased souls, so that they are restored to the image of God in which we were created, Wesley thought that our salvation involved the gradual restoration of our relationships to the health that God intended for them. His comments about God restoring our relationships with creation and with ourselves show solid theological grounding for modern mission issues of creation care and mental health, even though these concepts did not exist until centuries after Wesley's time!

Seeing the restoration of relationship as an end goal of God's good news, as Wesley did, helps us see other connections between various distinct understandings of good news. When we look at our relations with others, we see that the good news of restored relationships is connected not only to the good news of freedom from sins but to the good news of resurrection as well. Think back to the interaction between Jesus and the lawyer that frames the story of the good Samaritan. The lawyer's initial question to Jesus is "What must I do to gain eternal life?" The discussion about loving your neighbor that follows is thus a discussion about eternal life. For Jesus, the good news of relationship is directly connected to the good news of eternal life! Moreover, as we saw at the beginning of this chapter, restored relationships with the poor and marginalized are an important facet of the good news of the kingdom of God. These links are

---

5   See Randy L. Maddox, *Responsible Grace: John Wesley's Practical Theology* (Nashville: Kingswood Books, 1994), 68.

an important reminder that although there are many dimensions to God's good news, there are important connections between all of them.

Thinking about our own lives, we can identify points where restored relationships were good news, whether or not we recognized these instances as the work of God. We might think about times when long-simmering family feuds were ended, when failing marriages were repaired, when wars came to an end, when we got over our anger and our disappointment with ourselves, and when we again felt God's presence in our lives after a long time without it. Such instances are indeed good news! As Christians, we should not only recognize God's role in such moments in our lives but also want others to experience such moments in ways that are most meaningful to them.

Wesley's list of the four types of human relationships really highlights how broad this category of good news is. It can involve everything from people's sense of connection to God, to how people interact with their families, to peace between tribes or nations, to people's efforts to conserve wildlife habitat, to the process of healing from mental illness. Accordingly, evangelism, spiritual development, peacemaking, social justice, social work, care of God's creation, drug addiction services, mental health counseling, education, and more can all be an expression of this dimension of God's good news. Actually, restored relationships should be part of all aspects of mission.

What's more, since mission itself is a form of relationship building, the very act of being in mission of any type is an expression of this dimension of God's good news! In our world, boundaries disrupt relationship. Yet by being in mission and cultivating relationships with others across boundaries, we repair our own broken relationships with those on the other side of human boundaries. The following chapter will have more to say about the intrinsic connection between mission and cultivating relationships across boundaries. For now, let us conclude by noting that mission is thus not only a process by which we offer the good news of restored relationship to others, it is a process by which we claim the good news of restored relationship for ourselves.

■ MISSION TAKEAWAYS

In this chapter, we've discussed a variety of biblical views on good news. What about these biblical views is important to keep in mind as we read through the rest of this book? What are the main insights for mission of this overview of biblical understandings of good news? We can identify three takeaways:

1. God's good news is central to Christianity. The Bible talks about good news in at least four distinct though related ways: as the kingdom of God, as freedom from sins, as resurrection, and as restoration of relationship. Within each of these four dimensions, there are multiple aspects or possible understandings of good news.

2. As Christians in mission, we are called to be messengers of God's good news. We do not, however, know the complete message of good news since the full extent of God's love and God's nature is beyond the ability of any human being to understand. Instead, we are called to share our knowledge of good news in conversation with others so that we may together come to a fuller understanding of God's good news.

3. Since God's good news is a broad and multifaceted message, we should expect mission, which expresses this good news, to take many forms. Many types of mission are legitimate expressions of God's good news. Just as there is not just one piece of good news, there is not just one type of mission. Yet all forms of legitimate mission should be connected to some aspect of God's good news.

■ DISCUSSION QUESTIONS

Use these questions to guide group study of this chapter or for individual reflection:

1. Share some good news you've recently received. How does it feel to give good news? How does it feel to receive good news?
2. In your own words, describe God's good news for you, your family, your church.
3. Are there aspects of good news presented in this chapter that you hadn't considered before? If so, what are your reactions to them?
4. Are there other aspects of good news not mentioned in this chapter that you associate with Christianity?
5. Which aspect(s) of good news has (have) been most meaningful in your life?
6. Looking around your church and neighborhood, what kind of good news is needed most? Which aspect(s) of good news do you most associate with mission?
7. Are the aspects of good news that you find most personally meaningful and those you most associate with mission the same? Why do you think they align or don't align?
8. Think through the current mission work of your congregation. What aspect(s) of good news do you think is (are) most central to this work?
9. Think through the current mission work of your congregation. Do you believe that everyone involved has or needs the same understanding of good news?

■ FURTHER READING

Here are some other books related to topics in this chapter and why you should read them:

Mortimer Arias, *Announcing the Reign of God: Evangelization and the Subversive Memory of Jesus* (Lima, OH: Academic

Renewal Press, 2001). Arias's classic work on evangelism focuses on the kingdom (or reign) of God as the center of Jesus's message of good news and thus of great relevance for contemporary evangelism. He explores the breadth of meanings of the kingdom, including the other dimensions of good news discussed in this chapter.

Soong-Chan Rah, *The Next Evangelicalism: Freeing the Church from Western Cultural Captivity* (Downers Grove, IL: IVP Books, 2009). Rah's book uses the growth of immigrant and other nonwhite Christian populations in the United States to explore some of the ways in which white Western culture has distorted how American Christians understand their religion and the good news offered by Christianity.

Miriam Adeney, *Kingdom Without Borders: The Untold Story of Global Christianity* (Downers Grove, IL: IVP Books, 2009). Adeney uses personal stories of Christians from all around the world to demonstrate the many ways Christians find good news in Christianity. The book uses a combination of geographical and thematic approaches to present these stories.

Jaroslav Pelikan, *Jesus Through the Centuries: His Place in the History of Culture* (New Haven, CT: Yale University Press, 1999). Pelikan offers eighteen different titles for and descriptions of Jesus in an effort to describe how people at various points throughout history have understood him (and his good news) from within their own contexts.

4 Relates Well to Others

"Love each other like the members of your family.
Be the best at showing honor to each other. . . .
Consider everyone as equal, and don't think that
you're better than anyone else. Instead, associate with
people who have no status." (Romans 12: 10, 16a)

From Doing to Relating

When we understand mission as helping, it's easy to think of mission as something that we do, a program with prescribed actions that we undertake. As long as we perform the right sort of actions (i.e., actions that help other people), then we can feel good about having engaged in mission. Who is being helped and whether those actions are onetime or ongoing is irrelevant. Mission in this view is mission, regardless of whether it happens one time or weekly, regardless of whether it happens with people we will only ever see once or people we will see regularly.

Moreover, when we think about mission as helping, it is easy to think of mission as a verb that requires a direct object. That is, we think of mission as an action we do to someone, or perhaps for someone. That person or those people become the objects of our mission. They are not seen as subjects, as people capable of doing themselves; instead, they are seen as objects, as the recipients of our good works. We tend to see ourselves as the sole actors in mission as helping.

The impact of our actions may be seen as irrelevant as well, if what really counts is the doing itself. We tend to focus on the program and not the outcome. If we hand out bags of groceries, then we have done mission, even if those receiving the bags of groceries throw away half of the contents once they've walked around the corner. I occasionally volunteered at a large food pantry in Boston where this happened—leaving from my shift, I would see strewn about the sidewalk the unpopular items from the bags of groceries, the contents of which the recipients had no control over. Because I also volunteered at another food pantry where customers could choose their food, I knew that the food was thrown away not from carelessness or ingratitude. It was thrown away because those receiving it could not cook it or did not want to eat it because it did not fit with their cultural diet. What would you do if you were given several free bags of fried crickets? Yet when we are focused on the program and not the impact, even amid discarded groceries we may say that we have done our part—the rest is up to the recipients.

Such a temptation to see mission as doing, as action, is natural for United Methodists. Wesleyan theology emphasizes an active faith. While John Wesley always affirmed that our salvation comes through faith imparted by God's grace alone, he was also clear that God's gracious love enables and requires a response on our part. Because God loves us, we are also called to love God and others. And for Wesley, loving God and others meant keeping busy. He instructed his preachers, "Never while away time, nor spend more time at any place than is strictly necessary."[1] He disputed the Moravians (who were no slouches when it came to mission) and "Quietists" over recommendations

---

1   John Telford, "The Life of John Wesley," Wesley Center Online, http://wesley.nnu.edu/john-wesley/the-life-of-john-wesley-by-john-telford

that individuals not do good works until after they were wholly converted. Wesley wanted people to start doing good works as soon as possible! Wesley's whole theological approach has been described as "practical," that is, oriented toward doing things.

We American Methodists have a particularly strong bent toward action. Americans as a people have always been doers. We have always extolled those who worked hard, strived mightily, and accomplished great things. Americans admire those who *do* things, whether that is in business, science, the arts, or the church. American Christians of all theological persuasions tend toward the practical in their engagement with the world. We are not content to sit around and wait for God's kingdom to come; we are going to go out and make it happen!

Yet there are downsides to this attitude. When Americans travel around the world in mission, people from elsewhere repeatedly, and often with criticism, observe how task-oriented Americans are. Others see our preoccupation with projects as distracting us from other important values. Other theories of mission, such as those coming from continental Europe, have emphasized action and activism to a much lesser degree than have American views of mission. Instead of focusing on changing the world, European theories of mission stressed the devotional piety of Christians or the nature of the church as a community, its relation to individual Christians, and its relation to national communities.

> **Mission is not primarily something *we* do, it's something that *God* does.**

There are, however, benefits to a practical, action-oriented approach to the Christian faith. Schools are built. Diseases are cured. Disciples are made. Moreover, there are important differences between doing for and doing with. The latter approach exhibits a

/the-life-of-john-wesley-by-john-telford-chapter-14, accessed July 24, 2018.

commendable emphasis on mutuality between mission partners. Yet however conceived, there are some real potential problems with an action-oriented approach to mission if we let it distract us from the true nature of mission. If we see mission solely as the actions we do, especially if we see mission solely as actions that are part of some sort of program, we miss the mark in a couple of important ways.

First, when we think of mission as primarily constituted by our actions, we have missed the central insight that to the extent that mission does involve action, mission is not primarily something *we* do, it's something that *God* does. According to the principle of the *missio Dei*, mission begins with God. Mission may involve action on our part, but it starts with God's action. That recognition should put our own actions in perspective.

Second, seeing mission as actions overlooks the fundamentally relational nature of mission. As discussed in chapter 1, mission involves cultivating relationships across boundaries for the sake of fostering conversations in word and deed about the nature of God's good news. Mission may involve actions (or "deeds"), but it begins with relationship and makes relationship the end goal as well. It is relationship that makes cross-boundary conversations about God's good news possible. It is relationship, therefore, that undergirds whatever actions arise to express the insights of these conversations. Moreover, these relational conversations are not a means to accomplish something else. They are themselves the goal of mission.

Even when we focus on mission as "doing with" instead of "doing for," we too often emphasize the *doing* and not the *with*. We see relationships as means to an end, not the end itself. It is possible to affirm a "doing with" approach as the right way to do mission while still thinking of mission as primarily about accomplishing some set of projects. We may think that cultivating relationships is the best way to accomplish those projects without actually valuing those relationships for their own sakes. I am suggesting something stronger here. Relationship is not merely the best way to accomplish other objectives in mission. It should be our objective in mission.

As we saw in the previous chapter, restored relationship is one form of good news discussed in the New Testament. If our mission is to be about good news, then it cannot avoid being about relationship as an end of mission and not merely a means. If we attempt to practice mission without valuing relationship, we have already cut ourselves off from the fullness of God's good news. As those sent by God in mission, we must cultivate the restored relationships that God desires with humanity and that God desires humans to have with each other.

Mission and Love

Moreover, attention to the connection between mission and love helps us further see the relational nature of mission. Mission is an expression of love, both God's love for us and our love for God and for others. Love certainly involves actions—love that is not expressed is not love—but it is primarily about a *relationship*, not a task list. We love our family not just because they're people for whom we did something nice once, but because we have an ongoing pattern of interactions, emotional attachments, and reciprocal care. In other words, we love our families as part of ongoing relationships, not as a series of separate actions. Moreover, while there is room for intentionality and regularity in our relationships with our family, it would feel unnatural to confine our love for our family to a particular program of actions, say, perhaps serving them dinner (but not eating with them) every other Tuesday evening.

Another Wesleyan theological insight here tempers Wesley's emphasis on our active response to God's love. For Wesley, one of the primary ways in which his followers lived out their responsive love and grew in love for God and others was through their relationships with others. Wesley famously wrote, "The gospel of Christ knows of no religion, but social; no holiness but social holiness. Faith working by love, is the length and breadth and depth and height of Christian perfection."[2] When Wesley wrote about "social holiness," he wasn't referring primarily to social justice or to small-group devotional practices. He was referring to the importance of practicing love in relationships with real, concrete people.[3] It is impossible to love people in the abstract. One can only truly love specific people with whom one interacts. Small-group ministries can be an important means for structuring such interactions and an important means of mutual accountability, but it is clear that Wesley had in mind here a wide range of relationships, not just those with other Christians, let alone just other Methodists.

Thus, when we think about our church's mission efforts, the first question we ask ourselves should not be "What should we *do* for mission in our church?" It should be "Whom should we *relate to* in mission at our church?" It is even better if your church can ask not merely, "What individuals should the individuals in our church relate to?" but "What other communities should the community of our church relate to?" Missional relationships are most transformative (for us and others) when they occur not just with individuals but with entire networks. This shift from program-based mission thinking to relationship-based mission thinking is one of the most fundamentally important changes a congregation can make in its approach to mission.

This notion that mission is first and foremost about relationships may be challenging, especially to Americans. While individuals may differ, American culture often does not value

---

2   John Wesley, *Hymns and Sacred Poems* (1739), Preface, page viii, quoted in Steve Manskar, "No Holiness but Social Holiness," *Equipping Disciples*, https://blog.umcdiscipleship.org/no-holiness-but-social-holiness /#_ftn2, accessed July 24, 2018.

3   See chapter 2 of David N. Field, *Bid Our Jarring Conflicts Cease: A Wesleyan Theology and Praxis of Church Unity* (Nashville: Wesley's Foundery Books, 2017), for a good argument about the essentially relational nature of Wesley's concept of social holiness/social religion.

relationships as much as it does other things. It values money; it values material possessions; it values independence; it values achievement. Yet each of these stands in tension with and can undercut relationships. Relationships take time and attention, and often, we find ourselves short of both. Perhaps, then, it is not surprising that Americans are increasingly lonely. The average American's number of close friends has dwindled in recent decades.[4] For us in particular, this relational understanding of mission highlights just how countercultural God's mission can be. Americans' lack of relationships also points to another truth about mission—our participation in mission is not just how we share God's good news; it is how we receive God's good news, too. Hearkening back to the good Samaritan, often we are the traveler, and allowing ourselves to be befriended is how we receive healing and life. Building relationships with others in mission doesn't just benefit others; it benefits us.

Relationship across Boundaries

It is difficult enough to think about mission as primarily about relationships instead of actions. Yet, participating in God's mission is even more difficult than just that. Not all relationships are equally relevant to mission. God's mission calls us not merely to form relationships, but to cross boundaries to form relationships with those who are different from us. This makes the challenge of God's mission that much harder.

---

4   On increased loneliness, see Rhitu Chatterjee, "Americans Are a Lonely Lot, and Young People Bear the Heaviest Burden," National Public Radio, (May 1, 2018), https://www.npr.org/sections/health-shots /2018/05/01/606588504/americans-are-a-lonely-lot-and-young -people-bear-the-heaviest-burden, accessed July 24, 2018. On decreased number of friends, see "Americans Have Fewer Friends Outside the Family, Duke Study Shows," *Duke Today* (June 23, 2006), https://today.duke.edu/2006/06/socialisolation.html, accessed July 24, 2018.

To the extent that we have relationships, they are probably with people who are similar to us: people of our same race, same social class, same religious beliefs, same political views, etc. Research has shown that people even tend to form friendships with people who have a similar level of attractiveness![5] For Americans, the trend of surrounding themselves with people who are predominantly like them has increased in recent decades, driven by increased mobility, among other factors.[6] New technologies have reinforced our tendencies toward self-selection and self-segmentation. We now use social media to surround ourselves with the voices and views of those who are similar to us.

Yet Jesus makes it clear that we must love more than just the members of our own in-group. In the Sermon on the Mount, he says, "If you love only those who love you, what reward do you have? Don't even the tax collectors do the same? And if you greet only your brothers and sisters, what more are you doing? Don't even the Gentiles do the same? Therefore, just as your heavenly Father is complete in showing love to everyone, so also you must be complete" (Matthew 5:46-48). Those who are like us, those who already love us, certainly deserve our love, but our love must not stop there. The last verse, rendered in the King James Version as "Be ye therefore perfect, even as your Father which is in heaven is perfect," was foundational for Wesley's theology of sanctification. For Wesley, developing spiritually meant not only growing in love for others, but growing in love for others who are different from you.

Think back to the parable of the good Samaritan. Part of the power of the parable is not just that the Samaritan befriends the traveler or that the traveler accepts the Samaritan's care, it's that this relationship happens despite the significant divisions between

5   April Bleske-Rechek and Melissa Lighthall, "Attractiveness and Rivalry in Women's Friendships with Women," *Human Nature* 21 No. 1 (March 2010), 82-97.

6   Bill Bishop, *The Big Sort: Why the Clustering of Like-Minded America Is Tearing Us Apart* (Boston, MA: Mariner Books, 2009).

the two communities they come from. Jews and Samaritans had a lot of enmity between each other, yet the Samaritan befriended the Jewish traveler, despite those differences. Their relationship crossed boundaries. That is true love.

If we look at the history of Christian mission, it is obvious that such mission could not have occurred without the willingness to engage with people who were different from those Christians sent out in mission. Without a willingness to engage with people who were different, Paul and Peter would never have conducted mission with the Gentiles. Christianity would have remained a subset of Judaism. The same is true for every cultural, geographic, economic, political, and ethnic boundary that has been crossed by Christians in mission since then. If Christians were not willing to cross boundaries for the sake of mission, Christianity would have remained confined to a small group of Mediterranean Jews and would eventually have withered, rather than becoming the vibrant, growing, worldwide faith that it is today.

There are many types of boundaries that Christians can cross in mission nowadays. Those boundaries include cultural, economic, racial, gender, ethnic, political, linguistic, religious, and more types. These boundaries operate on a variety of geographic scales. We can cross these boundaries locally, within our home countries, or internationally. Although the set of boundaries might be different in each setting, boundaries exist in every setting. Whether we are engaged in local, domestic, or international mission, it is clear we must be crossing boundaries for the sake of mission.

The next chapter will explore in greater detail the nature of the boundaries that we cross and how we can best understand these boundaries and their impact on the nature of mission and our understandings of good news. The remainder of this chapter will examine some general guidelines for how to go about establishing relationships across boundaries, whatever and wherever those boundaries may be.

Love Your Neighbor as Yourself

Remember, Jesus's boundary-crossing parable of the good Samaritan came in response to a discussion of the greatest commandments. The second commandment that the legal expert presented, and Jesus affirmed, is "Love your neighbor as yourself." It's a classic Christian (and Jewish) teaching, but it holds a lot of depth. After all, questions about the interpretation of this teaching set up the story of the good Samaritan.

Given the placement of the parable of the good Samaritan within a discussion about this commandment, it makes sense to consider what the commandment has to say about forming relationships across boundaries. First and foremost, if we are to love our neighbors as ourselves, we must value our neighbors as we do ourselves. We must recognize their full humanity, humanity that is on par with our own. We must see them as equals with ourselves, or we do not love them as we love ourselves. Loving someone as you love yourself implies equality between you and them.

Remember the discussion of compassion vs. pity in the chapter on the good Samaritan. The good Samaritan helped the traveler because he had compassion on the traveler, not pity. He recognized the traveler as a fellow human. The good Samaritan understood that he could easily have been in the traveler's situation. That recognition of a common humanity and the fundamental equality between the good Samaritan and the traveler is what allowed the good Samaritan to have compassion on the traveler, to love him.

The recognition of our equal humanity with those with whom we are in mission is not only a prerequisite for mission; it may also be one of the best outcomes of mission. It restores relationships among humans. It can also restore the image of God in people who have suffered a long time from prejudice and condescension. Mark, a man who had come into contact with the United Methodist–run Community Hope Center in Florida, remarked of his experiences with that organization, "Before, people treated me like I was just a number, but when I came here, it's not that you gave me food or even helped me find a house—it's that you made me feel like a person, you made me feel real."[7] For Mark, the best news, better than overcoming homelessness, was having his humanity recognized by others. The staff at Community Hope Center loved Mark by seeing him as a human, equal to themselves.

Moreover, recognizing others' humanity does not diminish but rather enhances our own. When we see others with all their strengths and weaknesses as fully human, it frees us to be honest about our own weaknesses as well as our strengths. We need not always put on a false face toward the world, pretending that we have it all together. We can be fully human, with all the wonderful and challenging parts that entails.

The Myth of Meritocracy

It is often difficult, however, for Christians to recognize themselves as equals with those with whom they are in mission. This is especially true for Christians who are American, well-to-do, and/or white. Americans are taught that they live in a meritocracy. Those who do better in life deserve to do better. Those who do worse in life deserve to do worse. Moreover, the primary measure of whether one does better or worse is one's level of wealth and social status. Therefore, the well-to-do aren't just fortunate; we see them as *better* than the poor because they deserve their wealth. The poor aren't poor just because they have been misfortunate; we think they *deserve* to be poor because of their misdeeds, flaws, and/or shortcomings. This sort of thinking is deep-seated in the American psyche, but it represents a huge barrier to engaging in true and effective mission.

---

7   Amber Feezor, "Ministry With: Community Hope Center," General Board of Church and Society, https://www.umcjustice.org/news-and-stories /ministry-with-community-hope-center-659, accessed May 16, 2018.

It is difficult, when operating with such assumptions, to see a shared humanity between rich and poor, between have and have-not. It is difficult to believe, as the good Samaritan did of the traveler, that "there, but for the grace of God, go I." In this view, the rich (or middle class) could never have been poor, at least not for long. Their wealth demonstrates their superiority, and their superiority means that they were destined to inevitably rise to the top because they possess the right stuff. By contrast, in this view, it was also inevitable that the poor would end up poor because they lacked the right stuff to succeed. One's economic and social position is seen as a direct expression of one's morality, intellect, and abilities. The well-to-do are "winners," and the poor are "losers," and the difference between the two is fundamental.

With such a mindset, well-to-do Christians see the poor only as deficits, problems, and needs, whereas they see themselves as assets, successes, and abilities. In other words, well-to-do Christians do not see the poor as fundamentally equal to them. They see the poor as inherently less than themselves. While the well-to-do may recognize some level of humanity in the poor, it is not qualitatively the same sort of humanity as that possessed by the well-to-do. With such views, well-to-do Christians may have pity on the poor, but they cannot have compassion, since they are unable to imagine themselves in the situation of the poor.

The "solution" in this view of poverty is to make the poor more like the well-to-do, to "help" them change their nature, which is seen as defective. Yet what type of love forces someone else to be like you? If a boyfriend or girlfriend wanted their significant other to dress the same as them, to like the same types of food, hobbies, books, and movies, etc., regardless of whatever their actual preferences were, to have the same friends and no others, then we wouldn't applaud them for how loving they were. Instead, we would identify that boyfriend or girlfriend as controlling and manipulative. Yet how often have well-to-do Christians acted like manipulative boyfriends and girlfriends toward those we claim to love and want to help! We must do better.

The Impact of Stereotypes and Implicit Biases

When such views about the poor are combined with implicit assumptions about the superiority of whites over persons of color, the inability to fully empathize and recognize the humanity of others is that much greater. Note that I am not talking here about explicit, consciously held bias toward people of color. Instead, I am talking about the sorts of implicit biases and stereotypes that our culture imparts to even well-meaning persons who would never consciously do something racist. When the first associations one has for blacks, Hispanics, and other people of color are negative ones—poverty, crime, broken families, drugs, moral failings, etc.—it is difficult for white people to presume a fundamental equality between themselves and people of color, since such negative connotations do not exist for being white. The racism of American culture proclaims that whites and people of color are fundamentally different from each other. Whether or not one consciously agrees with such statements, we are all cognitively and emotionally affected by them. Research has consistently shown that such implicit biases can affect the behavior even of those who aspire to treat everyone equally.[8]

Such stereotypes of people based on race, ethnicity, and nationality can apply both within the US and internationally. Americans of all races, but especially white Americans, are taught by culture some deep-seated stereotypes about people from other countries, especially developing nations. We can assume that people living in developing nations are poor because of personal shortcomings. We see them as lazy, stupid, or corrupt. Such prejudiced views have a long history in Western culture. They become the lenses through which we see others, and those lenses are self-reinforcing. If we assume people from developing countries are lazy, then we will look for signs of laziness, and

8   "Implicit Bias," UCLA Equity, Diversity and Inclusion, https://equity.ucla .edu/know/implicit-bias/, accessed July 24, 2018.

when we see such signs, even in one individual, they serve as proof that our biases were right in the first place. Yet when we see contrary evidence of hardworking people, we dismiss it because it does not fit with our assumptions. Furthermore, these thought processes can happen subconsciously, without our even being aware that we are making such judgments. Such judgments can be further reinforced by cultural misunderstandings of how work is structured and carried out in other societies.

Nor is it only economic class, race, or nationality that we have stereotypes around. And such implicit biases are by no means only held by Americans. This is a shared problem for people everywhere. No matter who we are and how we define the "other," we have assumptions about what "those people" are like and how they are different from us. Such stereotypes prevent us from recognizing our shared humanity with the other. We assume that we are different from them not because of accidents of birth or circumstance, but because of real, deep-seated differences in our natures. When we have such prejudices against others, we cannot love them as ourselves, since we cannot recognize them as fellow humans who are fully like ourselves.

Again, whether or not we consciously embrace such views, they still affect how we think about our relationships with others around the world, including others with whom we are in mission. Even when we reject such stereotypes, their existence impacts our ability to empathize and identify with those who are stereotyped. We inherit these implicit biases, not because of anything we do but because they are in the cultural air we breathe. Indeed, implicit biases work best when we are unaware of them.

Thus, an important part of engaging in building relationships across boundaries is confronting and overcoming our biases, whether explicit or implicit. Such work is slow, difficult, and long-term, but vitally necessary if we are to develop true, reciprocal, and equal relationships between ourselves and others, the types of relationships called for in God's mission. Fortunately, there are ways in which we can go about overcoming even our implicit biases. Books such as Christena Cleveland's *Disunity in Christ* can be great resources.[9]

Overcoming such biases doesn't mean denying our differences from others. In fact, as the next chapter will show, it is very important to recognize such differences. Differences are important parts of who we are. If part of loving ourselves means accepting ourselves for who we are, then we must also acknowledge who others are and accept them as such. That includes acknowledging how people are different from us and accepting those differences as part of who they are.

Although we should not deny our differences with others, overcoming our biases does, however, mean that we no longer believe such differences stem from a fundamental level of others' being. Instead, we recognize our common humanity, a humanity that expresses itself in a variety of cultural, political, ethnic, racial, gender, and other configurations, but is not fundamentally divided by these differences. We recognize difference without letting it get in the way of seeing others as equals.

Once we can fully recognize our differences and affirm our common humanity with others despite those differences, then we can be fully in relationship with others. We can recognize that others, like ourselves, have assets to bring to a relationship. We can recognize that others, like ourselves, are able to think, to reason, to feel. We can recognize that others operate with the same degree of rationality and the same mix of motives that we do. We can recognize that others, like ourselves, have a desire to be loved and understood. We can begin the process of learning about others—their hopes and dreams, their joys and pains, how they understand the world and themselves. When this happens, we are in mission together.

---

9   Christena Cleveland, *Disunity in Christ: Uncovering the Hidden Forces That Keep Us Apart* (Downers Grove, IL: IVP Books, 2013).

Show Up, Shut Up, and Listen

The emotional and cognitive work that is involved in overcoming our biases and stereotypes is important, but it does not answer practical questions about how we go about forging relationships with those who are different from us. This section will attempt to offer such guidance by providing ten suggestions for building relationships.

1. Be in it for the long haul. Relationships take time and effort. That time and effort must be sustained over weeks, months, years, even decades. If you are considering cultivating a missional relationship, ask yourself, am I able to commit to this relationship for the long-term? Am I willing to take the time to cultivate relationships? Am I willing to put in the emotional work that goes with being in relationship with others? Am I willing to be inconvenienced and even to sacrifice for the sake of relationship with others? For Americans, making such commitments goes against the grain of American culture. Jesus's comments in Luke 14:28-32 about counting the cost beforehand are an appropriate caution we should take to heart.

In addition to asking ourselves whether we are willing to put in the necessary time and work, we should also ask ourselves whether we are willing to stick with these missional relationships, even when they are challenging. All relationships go through cycles of growth and tension. All relationships involve conflicting expectations and resultant disappointments at times. All relationships involve one or the other party making mistakes at times. Commitment to be in a missional relationship means commitment to stick with that relationship through the tensions, disappointments, and mistakes—the other party's and our own—that inevitably characterize relationships.

These warnings don't mean that you can never make changes in your mission relationships if situations shift. They do mean, however, that you should not treat the process of relationship cultivation casually. If you know you can't be in it for the long haul, don't do it. If you start creating a relationship but can't follow through, you will only leave hurt on the part of the other when you withdraw from that relationship.

2. Build on existing connections. When we as churches are looking to build missional relationships, we rarely work from scratch. We usually build new relationships by leveraging existing connections. Those connections may be to individuals, to communities, to places, or to organizations. In the Fresh Expressions movement, missional leaders look for "persons of peace," people who can serve as gateways to a community and provide the opportunity to begin building relationships with that community.[10] Other relationships in the community are built from an initial relationship with that person of peace. Whether you are working locally or elsewhere, it is important to identify the persons of peace who will open relational doors for you and your church.

Such connections may not be shared by all members of a congregation. They may be specific to one or two people, and part of the challenge of developing missional relationships can be discovering who in a congregation has existing connections that can be leveraged. When such connections are identified, then they can become the basis for more connection—more extensive connections, more people in the church who participate in the connection, and ultimately connections to more people outside the church. Again, the best missional relationships are between communities and not just among individuals.

3. Hang out. Relationships are built through spending time together. There are lots of ways to spend time together and lots of excuses for doing so. Find one that works for you, your church, and those with whom you are developing relationships. Then use that excuse to hang out, regularly. The more unstructured the interaction, the better, as it allows relationship-deepening interactions to happen on their own time in their own way. Remember, the goal is to develop relationships, not programs.

---

10 See Kenneth H. Carter Jr. and Audrey Warren, *Fresh Expressions: A New Kind of Methodist Church for People Not in Church* (Nashville: Abingdon Press, 2017), 108-9.

One particular form of hanging out you may wish to consider is offering and receiving hospitality. Hospitality includes, among other aspects, visiting one another and eating together. Eating together can be a powerful form of relationship building. It is a perfect unstructured form of interaction. Note that when you are engaging in hospitality, whether that is visiting one another or eating together, it is important to be willing to both give and receive. The goal is to foster mutual relationships. Relationships can't be mutual, however, if they always occur on one person's or one group's turf. If one side is always host and one side is always guest, that creates inequality, which hampers relationship.

4. Don't let work get in the way. Working together on a project can be a good reason to spend time together and a way to cooperatively improve the world. Yet it's important that the means don't become ends in and of themselves. Americans, in particular, have a tendency to be task-oriented rather than relationship-oriented. There is a danger that focusing on completing a task can lead to relationships being ignored or even harmed.

Such a danger is especially high for domestic and international mission trips. Even when congregations travel to the same spot repeatedly, the nature of such trips makes these relationships episodic. Participants and hosts usually see each other once a year. (Regular Skype calls for prayer and fellowship between trips can be a good way to make such relationships more regular.) Moreover, there is usually some identified work objective that justifies the trip. Church members going on the trip may feel it is critical to complete that objective. Yet there are numerous stories of trips where the hosts felt overlooked or insulted because their American guests cared more about painting a wall than they did getting to know and spend time with their hosts. The work is always there; the chance to build relationships is not.

I have a friend whose father would only come to visit her if there was some sort of home repair that he could help her with. She would therefore find things around her home to fix just so her dad would visit. While visiting, he would spend most of his time fixing things rather than spending time with her, and when he was done, he would go home again. This was an unsatisfying relationship for my friend; she wanted a fuller relationship with her father. Americans on mission trips often act like my friend's dad, though. We come only when there is something we can do, we spend all of our time doing it instead of relating, and when it's done, we go home. The relationships that are forged in this way are just as unsatisfying to our hosts as the relationship with her father is to my friend.

5. Listen, listen, listen. If your goal is to get to know others as part of a deep and meaningful relationship, there is no short-cut for listening to them. We get to know others when we listen. Listening is often a lost skill, especially in contemporary society where we are focused on promoting ourselves and advocating for our own beliefs. Yet, as the old adage says, God gave us two ears and only one mouth for a reason. To build relationships, we must pray, as in the prayer attributed to St. Francis, to seek not so much to be understood as to understand. We must be willing to honestly share about ourselves, especially when asked. But listening must be our default posture. It is a primary way of showing respect for and openness to others.

6. Listen first, judge later (if at all). How we listen is just as important as that we listen. There is a difference between listening to evaluate and listening to understand. If we are listening to evaluate, then we are always comparing what others say about themselves to our own beliefs, standards, opinions, and preferences. Some such comparison is natural for human cognition, but when this becomes the focus of our listening, the result is not relationship, but judgment. It is inevitable that others will differ from us in some ways that will touch on important beliefs and convictions we have. Yet relationships are best served if we can shift from asking ourselves, "Is what I am hearing good or bad?" to asking ourselves "Why are they saying that?" Making the primary goal of listening understanding rather than judgment is incredibly beneficial to relationship.

It also means that, if we must eventually make judgments about others, we can do so with full information and a sufficiently nuanced approach to interpreting others' beliefs, actions, and motivations. We can practice discernment instead of judgment. Discernment is more about cultivating wisdom and understanding, whereas judgment is about categorization into good and bad. By focusing on categorization, judgment reinforces rather than crosses boundaries. Discernment, on the other hand, puts human boundaries into the perspective of divine truths about our common humanity and God's universal love.

7. Be yourself. Just because you are developing relationships with others who are different from you doesn't mean that you have to hide who you are. Being yourself is a form of honesty. Don't lie to other people; it does not lead to healthy long-term relationships built on trust. If you want to get to know others, you have to be willing to let others get to know you. If you want to fully recognize and understand who they are and how they understand the world, you need to be honest about who you are and how you see the world. That doesn't mean you need to be confrontational in highlighting differences. That certainly doesn't mean insisting that your way is better. It's always best to show respect. That does mean, however, being honest about yourself, even when there are differences between yourself and others.

8. Be brave! One of the reasons why we tend to hide who we are when we interact with others who are different from us is that we fear rejection. Yet to develop real relationships with others, we must be willing to brave the risk of such rejection. Author Brené Brown has written about the importance of being oneself, including being comfortable with one's shortcomings, for the process of establishing connection.[11] It is only when we are willing to face our fears of rejection and take emotional risks that we can really establish relationships. We must be willing to be vulnerable for the sake of establishing connections, even when

---

11 Brené Brown, *The Gifts of Imperfection*.

that vulnerability feels risky. Avoiding vulnerability can manifest as attempts to avoid awkwardness, failure, embarrassment, etc., but these experiences are all part of the process of mission. We should embrace rather than avoid them.

9. Make it not about you. Did you ever have a friend who always seemed to want your friendship to be on their terms? When we have friends who always insist on their own agendas as part of our friendships with them, we feel hurt and used. Such friendships never flourish. As Christians in mission, we must be wary to avoid falling into this trap. When we are seeking to develop missional relationships, we must take care that our own agendas, our own plans, our own hopes for missional partnerships arising from relationships not get in the way of those relationships. We must be prepared for those with whom we are developing relationships to have their own agendas, plans, hopes, and dreams. We must allow our relationships to be shaped just as much, if not more so, by those other peoples' agendas, plans, hopes, and dreams as our own. We must try to see the relationship not only from our own perspective, but from the perspective of the other. In other words, we must be willing to give and take.

10. Demonstrate that you care. Good relationships involve caring for each other, and that care is often acted out in concrete ways. Therefore, there is a place for actions in a mission based on relationships. Yet these actions are a secondary rather than a primary part of mission, and they need not be part of a formal program. Actions flow from relationship and serve to build up that relationship; they are not ends in and of themselves. Put in proper perspective, actions can be a critical means by which we demonstrate that we have listened and understood others and their hopes and dreams. Actions as the fruit of relationships can be important for demonstrating to others the extent of our care for them. When we act in this way, we act as messengers of God's good news as part of God's mission.

■ MISSION TAKEAWAYS

This chapter has had a lot to say about relationships and the attitudes and practices that support them. What is most important to keep in mind about relationships as we are engaging in mission? We can identify three takeaways:

1. Focus on relating, not doing, in mission. Mission does not consist primarily of actions or programs. Actions are the fruit of missional relationships. Relationship building, with entire communities as well as individuals, must be the primary focus of and basis for mission.

2. Develop relationships across difference. Mission must involve a willingness to engage with those who are different from you and your community in some significant way. This principle applies to local, domestic, and international mission.

3. Love your neighbor as yourself. Recognize your common humanity with your neighbor, acknowledging but not essentializing your differences. Then be prepared to show up, shut up, and listen to build relationships founded on honesty and understanding.

■ DISCUSSION QUESTIONS

Use these questions to guide group study of this chapter or for individual reflection:

1. In your opinion, what characterizes a strong relationship? How is a casual friendship different from a significant or best friendship?

2. What close relationships do you currently have with people outside your church and your immediate family? What are these relationships like?

3. Can you think of a time in your own life when you were focused too much on tasks and not enough on relationships? What were the consequences?

4. Think about a time in your life that you felt deeply listened to. What was that experience like? What did the other person do (or not do) that made you feel so well-listened to? What is it like when someone won't listen to you?

5. This chapter makes a strong case for overcoming our class, racial, national, and other biases, even when these are implicit rather than consciously held. What is your reaction to this argument? Do you agree that such biases can hinder the process of forming relationships?

6. What relationships are crucial to your current mission programs? What relationships could your current mission programs not run without? (If you cannot answer this question, it is time to seriously reconsider your mission programs!) What are those relationships like? Are they equal relationships?

7. What boundaries are crossed in your current mission work? What does that boundary crossing look like? How relational is that boundary crossing?

8. What types of new relationships do you think God is calling you and your congregation to develop? Why do you think God is moving you and your congregation in this direction?

■ FURTHER READING

Here are some other books related to topics in this chapter and why you should read them:

Dana L. Robert, *Faithful Friendships: Embracing Diversity in Christian Community* (Grand Rapids, MI: William B. Eerdmans Publishing Company, forthcoming in 2019). Robert shows how boundary-crossing friendships are a challenging but necessary part of Christian faith and mission. Using examples of cross-cultural friendships from mission history, she shares reflections on the practice of such friendships today.

Christena Cleveland, *Disunity in Christ: Uncovering the Hidden Forces That Keep Us Apart* (Downers Grove, IL: IVP Books, 2013). Cleveland combines social psychology and theology to explain why we so often separate ourselves from Christians who are different from us and how we can go about overcoming our innate biases to establish relationships that reflect the common identity we have in Christ.

Michael P. Nichols, *The Lost Art of Listening: How Learning to Listen Can Improve Relationships*, 2nd Edition (New York: The Guilford Press, 2009). Nichols identifies common obstacles to listening well and attentively to others, including a preoccupation with our own needs, hidden assumptions about others, and emotional defensiveness. Then he explains how to overcome these barriers, including specific listening exercises. While the book is geared toward listening to family members, friends, and coworkers, the lessons are applicable in mission relationships as well.

Brené Brown, *The Gifts of Imperfection: Let Go of Who You Think You're Supposed to Be and Embrace Who You Are* (Center City, MN: Hazelden Publishing, 2010). Brown lifts up courage, compassion, and connection as the results of living in a way that she terms "wholehearted." She suggests ten practices that allow for this type of wholehearted living characterized by greater self-love and love of the other.

5 Taking Our Differences Seriously

"Peter said, 'I really am learning that God doesn't show partiality to one group of people over another.'" (Acts 10:34)

And Now for Something Completely Different

In the last chapter, we saw how mission involved cultivating relationships across boundaries. That chapter provided some suggestions for how to go about pursuing such relationships, but this chapter will further expand on that process, especially the role that difference plays in establishing relationships across boundaries.

Put simply, while we must always affirm our common humanity with those among whom we are in mission, we should not underestimate the significance of the differences between us and others when we are seeking to form missional relationships. Instead, we must take those differences seriously, be mindful of them, and reflect on how they shape the nature of our relationships and each partner's perception of God's good news.

Again, that is not to say that when we form relationships across differences that we have nothing in common with those who are different from us. People are still people, no matter who they are, and sometimes surprising points of connection can be found between people from very different backgrounds and situations. Our differences in no fashion take away from our common humanity. I emphasized in the last chapter that recognizing that common humanity is critical for our ability to form healthy mission relationships.

You cannot love people in the abstract. Likewise, you can't do mission in the abstract.

Nor am I saying that we should stereotype people based on the differences we first perceive between them and us. The goal of relationship is to move beyond stereotyped and overly simplified understandings of other people. Such understandings are not helpful to true relationship and are instead harmful. Again, I emphasized in the last chapter that stereotypes and implicit biases detract from our ability to recognize our common humanity with others.

I am, however, saying that we shouldn't just dismiss the ways in which people are different from us with an attitude of "everyone is the same deep down, so differences don't really matter." This approach downplays the significance of real differences in favor of emphasizing projected similarities. Such an attitude may at times be well-intentioned, but it can prevent us from really understanding others. We impose on them our way of seeing the world instead of trying to understand them on their own terms. Moreover, such an attitude can be perceived as quite offensive by others when we tell them that core parts of their identity "don't really matter."

You may have grown up in a city or suburb, may not be from the Midwest, and probably have little to no experience with Norwegian-Americans. In those ways, you and I would be different from each other. You might tell me that these differences in our situations growing up aren't important. In many ways you might be right. But at some point, if you really want to know and understand who I am, you need to understand how my experiences growing up in a small town in the Midwest surrounded by Norwegian-Americans shaped who I am. Indeed, I wouldn't be writing this book if I didn't have that background. To simply dismiss the differences in where we grew up and write them off as not important would also be to dismiss an important part of me and how I see the world.

The same applies for all our relationships with other people. Part of being human is being different from others. These differences come in many forms, which we'll talk about below. Whatever their nature, our differences from other people are part of what makes us who we are. If we are not willing to recognize and understand the ways in which others are different from us, we are not willing to understand them. If we dismiss the differences we have from others, we dismiss an important part of them. Put another way, we cannot understand other people without understanding their unique backgrounds, experiences, and situations in life that help make them who they are.

Putting Our Differences in Context

While every human has her or his own life experiences that are unique to her or him, we share many aspects of our backgrounds and situations in life with others. My brothers and I have distinct personalities and life experiences, but we also share a family background and a hometown. Those shared elements make us similar to each other in some ways, even as they also make us different from others who do not share our family of origin or hometown. In the same way, my wife and I have shared the same family, living place, social circles, and economic situation over the course of our marriage. We have these things in common with each other, even as they also make us different from others.

Therefore, if we want to understand others, it is important not only to understand what is unique to each person as an individual but also what commonalities groups of people share and how those commonalities shape the individuals in that group. Humans are a combination of our individual personalities and experiences and our shared backgrounds and situations in life. Getting to know others is both a process of getting to know them as individuals and a process of getting to know the settings from which they come. If we are focusing on getting to know an entire community and not just an individual, paying attention to shared backgrounds and situations in life across the community is inescapable.

There is a word that describes the setting in life from which people come: context. Context can be defined as the world people inhabit. There are many elements to context: social context, including gender, age, race, ethnicity, and class; cultural context, including language, worldview, and shared references; economic context, including income level, line of work, and economic system; political context, including political affiliations and form of government; family context; and historical context. Additional elements of context could probably be added to this list. My point here is not to be comprehensive but to suggest the complexity of context.

Context is closely related to the concept of culture. Culture includes the systems of shared behaviors, beliefs, values, symbols, and material objects by which groups make sense of the world and structure their common life. Culture is a broad but important concept for those who study mission. There has been much discussion within the study of mission about how culture affects groups' understanding of the Christian message and therefore the process of communicating that good news. This chapter draws significantly on that study.

Yet the concept of context is broader than just culture, since it also includes elements like economic and political systems that, while they may be connected to culture, cannot be reduced to culture. To give an example, consider the US states of South Dakota and North Dakota. These two states are very similar culturally, perhaps as similar as any two US states can be. Yet there are important economic differences between the two. South Dakota's economy involves more tourism than North Dakota's, since South Dakota has several nationally famous landmarks. North Dakota, on the other hand, has had a recent oil boom following the discovery of shale oil in the Bakken oil fields. While the Bakken oil boom brought low unemployment to North Dakota, it also brought a housing shortage and an increase in sex trafficking. This difference between the contexts of South Dakota and North Dakota has potential missional significance, even though it doesn't directly involve culture. Therefore, this book will discuss the broader concept of context, of which culture is an important part.

Two further remarks about context are important. First, just as there are many components to context (cultural, social, economic, political, etc.), there are also layers to context. Thus, one can speak about local, national, and international contexts. For example, extreme weather related to a changing climate has been an important part of the global context in recent years, but whether that means drought, flooding, or both varies between local contexts. Moreover, organizations can be their own contexts. Members of The United Methodist Church, the Evangelical Lutheran Church in America, and the Southern Baptist Convention could all live in the same town and hence share the same local, national, and international contexts, but have very different religious contexts, based on their denominations. The same is true for the companies for which people work, among other organizations.

Second, contexts are never static. Change is the one constant of life, and social, economic, political, cultural, religious, and other forms of change are happening all the time, everywhere. These changes produce changes in contexts. Thus, for example, while there have been many continuities in the context of living in Puerto Rico over the years, there have also been significant changes in that context in the last several years because of the economic crisis and hurricanes on the island. That's why history is an important part of context—those changes leave their traces. Yet we shouldn't assume that because something was true about a context a year ago or is true about a context now, it will continue to be true in the future. Understanding contexts is an ongoing process.

Contexts Matter

It is important to understand what a context is because contexts matter to mission in at least two ways. First, contexts impact how we develop missional relationships with others. As this chapter has been arguing, it is impossible to really know and understand someone unless we can understand them as part of their contexts. It is furthermore impossible to have a good relationship with someone whom we do not really know or understand. Therefore, if we want to develop good missional relationships with others, we must understand their contexts.

The checkout person in my college's cafeteria was a friendly older woman, much friendlier than initially seemed reasonable to me for someone who was probably not making much money and had to deal with college students occasionally trying to smuggle potted plants out of the dining hall. As I got to know her over the course of my college career, though, I learned that she was an immigrant from Soviet Russia. Social control there was strict, and food was often scarce. The first time she went to an American grocery store, she was overwhelmed by how much was on the shelves, and she cried. Knowing more about the context from which she came allowed me to see her as more than just a friendly cashier who was patient with unruly college students. It helped me understand a little bit of the range of thoughts and feelings related to food and freedom that she must have experienced in her work at an American college cafeteria. It allowed me to develop a relationship with her that went beyond a smile and a wave.

Second, contexts impact how we understand good news. Mission is not just about establishing relationships across differences but about engaging in conversations within those relationships about the nature of God's good news. As we saw in chapter 3, the Bible speaks about multiple dimensions of good news. Context can affect both which of those dimensions resonate most deeply with people and how they understand the nature of that dimension of good news.

Two examples can illustrate. As discussed in chapter 3, part of God's good news is the good news of the kingdom, which includes God's healing. Yet healing can mean something very different depending on how one's culture understands diseases. Western medicine, Indian Ayurvedic medicine, Chinese traditional medicine, and African traditions that understand disease as a result of witchcraft, all have very different accounts of what causes disease. Therefore, they would each understand the claim that Jesus heals very differently. Moreover, even within one system of understanding disease, the availability of other means to treat disease can impact how important a part of good news it is that Jesus heals. If someone lives in a country with universal, high-quality health care (a function of their economic and political contexts), the claim that Jesus heals is likely to be acknowledged but not seen as central to faith. If someone lives in a country with limited and rudimentary health care, the claim that Jesus heals may be seen as one of the best parts of God's good news.

Another aspect of God's good news is the hope for eternal life in heaven after death. Yet when Christianity first encountered many traditional cultures, whether medieval Germanic culture, early modern Chinese culture, or twentieth-century African cultures, context significantly shaped how this aspect of good news was received. All these cultures contained a hope of being reunited with ancestors, family, and other loved ones in the afterlife. The Christian claim that Christians went to a Christian heaven after death was understood as a claim that if people converted to Christianity, they could not be with their family members after death, since they believed them to be in some other realm of the afterlife. This was seen not as good news, but as bad news! Without understanding the beliefs about the afterlife that were part of those contexts, it would have been impossible for Christians to adequately converse with others about God's good news in a way that effectively conveyed its goodness.

The Theater Metaphor

The point here is not that one context or another is "right" or "wrong" or that one context allows us to truly understand God's good news while another doesn't. All contexts have elements that help them understand God's good news and elements that hinder their understanding. No human context has a monopoly on truth. That is not to say that all truth is relative; it is instead a reminder to be humble about our ability to fully comprehend all of who God is or what God is doing in the world and a reminder to respect the ability of others who are also made in the image of God to recognize God and God's actions in the world.

The great mission scholar Andrew Walls uses a vivid image to convey how all contexts (or cultures, as he is writing about) have some, though a limited, ability to understand the gospel. He compares the story of God's good news to a play and all cultures to seats in the theater. Each theater seat allows the person sitting in it to see the play. Everyone, therefore, is able to see what God is doing in the world. Yet each seat gives a different view of the play. Moreover, no seat allows the person sitting in it to see all of what is happening on stage. A piece of scenery or part of the curtain or the direction the actors are facing will all mean that no one sees everything. It is humanly impossible.

In the same way, every culture (or context) can perceive God's good news, but no two cultures (or contexts) will see that good news in quite the same way, and no one culture (or context) can understand all of God's good news.[1] This universal but limited ability to understand the good news is central to why mission is cultivating relationships across boundaries for the sake

---

1   Andrew F. Walls, *The Missionary Movement in Christian History: Studies in the Transmission of Faith* (Maryknoll, NY: Orbis Books, 1996), 43–44.

of fostering conversations in word and deed about the nature of God's good news. Through such conversations, both partners come to understand that good news more fully—they learn to see what the other one sees that they can't.

Know Thyself

If context is so important to the goal of mission, how then can we understand our contextual differences with others? The first step is to better understand one's own context and how it shapes one's view of the world and one's understanding of the good news. It is not just other people who have a context; each one of us has a context. We all sit in a theater seat, to continue Walls's metaphor, and it shapes our view of the play.

Some elements of our context are easy to identify. We can generally state our age, gender, family members, occupation, and the country in which we live. Most of these questions involve basic biographical facts about us. Answering such questions may be a first step in coming to recognize our own contexts, but there is much, much more involved. Understanding one's context is not primarily about knowing personal facts. It is about understanding how the facts about and experiences of our lives shape the way we see ourselves and the world.

Sometimes seemingly basic questions can get into tricky issues of identity and self-understanding that aid in this process. For some, such as military kids or immigrants, the question "Where are you from?" can be a complicated one. If you moved frequently as a military kid, what really counts as home? An immigrant may want to claim that they are from both their home country and the country to which they moved. Such complicated answers to these basic biographical questions thus might tell us something significant about how our experiences and connections shape how we understand ourselves. It is important to recognize and work through such complex questions of personal identity in order to understand one's context and its impact on how one sees the world. Yet answering even these more complicated questions is not the end of the road in understanding one's own context.

The really difficult part of understanding one's context is not in identifying various facts about one's context, or in being able to articulate one's sense of individual identity, but in understanding how those facts and elements of identity shape how one sees the world and how one understands God's good news for that world. Our contexts are like eyeglasses. We see the world through them, but most of the time, we are focusing on what we are looking at, not on our glasses. Yet our glasses critically shape how and what we see, even when we're not paying attention to them. In the same way, our contexts shape how we see the world and what we see in it, but most of the time we are not paying attention to their role in doing so.

Learning to recognize the impact of one's context on how one sees the world involves taking time to stop, pay attention to one's thoughts and feelings, and question one's assumptions about and reactions to other things in the world. Asking yourself "Why?" is a key practice here. "Why do I assume that is true?" "Why did that experience make me feel happy/sad/embarrassed/confused?" "Why does that news seem like good news to me?" Learning to see the role our backgrounds and experiences play in shaping our answers to such "why" questions is a significant step toward being able to understand the relationship between our context and our view of the world.

This process of coming to understand one's context and its impact on how one sees the world is greatly aided by the process of interacting with others who are different from you. Don't wait until you've got your context all figured out to start building relationships across difference. Those relationships can be a critical part of the process of coming to understand your own context. It's especially useful to ask yourself why you respond, assume, or place value in a particular way when you can note the different responses, assumptions, and values that others bring to the same or a similar situation.

Then the question can become not just "Why do I do this?" but "Why do I do this and not that?" It can be tempting to answer the first question with "Because that's the only/best/most logical/most natural way to do it!" Seeing others who are doing things differently pushes us to think more deeply about why it is that we do things the way we do, especially when we assume that others, because of their common humanity with us, have the same degree of rationality and same mix of motivations that we do. Our actions flow not just from what's best/most logical/most natural in a universal sense, but from what's best/most logical/most natural within our context, which may be different than what's best/most logical/most natural in another context.

This process can be a difficult one. My brothers and I, despite sharing many relevant contexts, frequently have very different ideas about how to accomplish home repair projects. It can be tempting for each of us to assume that his way of doing things is the best and the fact that another brother wants to do it a different way means that he is obviously not thinking clearly or is missing some key piece of information. I have learned over the years to do the hard work of stopping to really listen to why one of my brothers wants to accomplish a shared task in their way. That listening doesn't always lead to agreement about the project, but it does generally help me understand what is motivating them and why I am coming at the shared project differently than they are, and it always benefits our relationship. If this process of trying to understand differing perspectives is difficult among my brothers and me, who love each other deeply and share a lot in common, it can be much more so between people from different cultures or countries. Yet the relational benefits are still there.

The process of coming to understand one's own context can therefore be difficult. It can, however, also be rewarding. In the last chapter, we discussed loving others as we love ourselves. By learning more about our contexts, we learn more about ourselves, and that opens us up to be able to love ourselves in new and deeper ways. We no longer need to base our self-love on a false notion that we have the complete truth and the absolute best way of doing things, which makes us worthy of love. Instead, we can love ourselves not because we think we're the best but because we know that God loves us no matter who we are. The first approach is a form of works righteousness. The second understands the centrality of God's grace. We can love ourselves, not because we are better/smarter/more reasonable than others. We can love ourselves because we are God's beloved creation. Such an insight is both more theologically profound and a more well-grounded sense of self-love.

Loving ourselves better in this way allows us to have greater humility. Humility is not about thinking poorly of ourselves, but of seeing ourselves rightly, with our good, bad, and indifferent attributes. Humility comes from a self-love that is based on understanding ourselves as shaped by our contexts, in their good, bad, and indifferent dimensions. It comes from understanding that there are negative aspects of our contexts and that we are limited by our contexts. While there may be vulnerability involved in admitting our weaknesses and negative aspects and those of our contexts, there is strength in this approach, too. When we don't have to pretend to be the best or pretend to be without flaws, then we can just be ourselves. Such vulnerable humility allows us to be more authentically ourselves when we interact with others.

When we interact with others, a posture of vulnerable, authentic humility allows us to be more open to them as well. Ideally, when we feel comfortable with who we are, then we can allow others to be themselves, too. We can see the good, bad, and indifferent in them and in their contexts, while knowing that this mix of good and bad does not determine God's love for them. We can love them more fully, not because they are the best or without flaws, but because we know God loves them as God's beloved creation, no matter who they are or what their strengths and weaknesses are. When we have experienced the power of

God's grace in the midst of our own admitted weaknesses and shortcomings, we are more willing to extend such grace to others.

Seeing Through Others' Eyes

Once we are on the journey to greater self-understanding and self-love by recognizing how our contexts have shaped us, we can also embark on the journey to greater other-understanding and other-love by recognizing how others' contexts have shaped them. There are several significant ways to learn more about the differences in context between ourselves and others and how these contextual differences can impact our relationships and our understandings of God's good news.

There is a wealth of material out there from both mission and business writers on culture and its impacts on how people understand the world and interact with one another. Reading some of this material can alert you to what to look for when learning about the cultural aspects of contextual differences. The work of Geert Hofstede and others inspired by his research has looked at cultural differences between countries and between organizations on issues such as how comfortable people are with overt power differences, how comfortable people are with uncertainty, whether decisions are made individually or collectively, and how people measure and relate to time.[2]

Understanding different attitudes toward time, for instance, can prevent a load of interpersonal misunderstanding and can open up some really interesting theological discussions.

---

2 Geert Hofstede wrote several books, perhaps most famously, *Cultures and Organizations: Software of the Mind: Intercultural Cooperation and Its Importance for Survival* (London: Profile Books, 2003). Among those inspired by Hofstede is Erin Meyer, *The Culture Map: Decoding How People Think, Lead, and Get Things Done Across Cultures* (New York: Public Affairs, 2014). For an online comparative resource based on Hofstede's work, see "Country Comparison," *Hofstede Insights*, https://www.hofstede-insights.com/country-comparison/, accessed September 6, 2018.

Americans, and Westerners generally, are very focused on clock time. Meetings should begin promptly, and schedules should be kept. Americans also speak of time using a variety of economic metaphors. We save, spend, or waste time. In much of the developing world, people are familiar with clock time, but it does not structure how people think of time to the same degree. Social events usually do not start promptly, and activities last as long as they take, rather than ending at some predetermined time. Relationships are more important than schedules. There is a sense that time is limitless, rather than a scarce quantity.

Differences in views of time between Americans and those in the developing world, if not fully understood or acknowledged, can cause relationship conflict. Americans can see those in the developing world as lazy or disorganized, whereas those in the developing world can see Americans as overly hurried, inconsiderate of others, and even disregarding of the Sabbath. Recognizing such differences and understanding that they do not necessarily reflect a "right" and a "wrong" view can help both sides move past such negative judgments toward acknowledging, accepting, and accommodating both perspectives.

Moreover, understanding such differences can even open up significant theological discussions that can help both sides better understand God's good news. How should we understand it, for example, when the Bible says that Jesus came in "the fullness of time" (Galatians 4:4 NRSV) or when Jesus says, "The time is coming" (repeatedly throughout the gospels, especially John)? Differing cultural perspectives on time will bring different approaches to interpreting such passages. Thus, sharing such differing views of time can enrich our mutual understandings of the scripture.

Culture is not the only component of context, though, and thus there are other ways in which to learn about how context shapes how people see the world. Much mission work involves relatively well-to-do Christians interacting with the poor in an attempt to "help" them. Ruby K. Payne and coauthors explore how differences in class context involve not only varying levels of money, but differences in values, priorities, skills, and orientations toward time, among others. The authors describe differences between the poor, middle class, and wealthy and show how each group has skills, abilities, and knowledge, and how these vary based on class context. They explain that understanding these differences is crucial to being able to work with others across class differences for the sake of effecting change.[3] Their insights are based on research in the United States and are most applicable there.

Jonathan Bonk has developed a thoughtful and often searing critique of the dangers of the economic differences between the context of Western missionaries and the poor around the world with whom they are in mission. While not everyone will be willing to follow the strongest of Bonk's recommendations to embrace poverty for ourselves, all would do well to listen to his warnings about the way in which differences in economic context can distort or even obscure the good news.[4]

Books that relate to understanding how one's racial context shapes one's experience of the world, including Debby Irving's *Waking Up White*,[5] can also be relevant resources for understanding one's own social and racial context, which can therefore help one to better understand others' context. Additional literature exists on other dimensions of contextual differences that apply predominantly in the United States—generational differences,[6]

---

3 Ruby K. Payne, Philip DeVol, and Terie Dreussi Smith, *Bridges Out of Poverty: Strategies for Professionals and Communities* (Highlands, TX: aha! Process, Inc., 2001). See especially chapter 3, "Hidden Rules Among Classes."

4 Jonathan J. Bonk, *Missions and Money: Affluence as a Western Missionary Problem* (Maryknoll, NY: Orbis Books, 1991).

5 Debby Irving, *Waking Up White: And Finding Myself in the Story of Race* (Cambridge, MA: Elephant Room Press, 2014).

6 Haydn Shaw, *Sticking Points: How to Get 4 Generations Working Together in the 12 Places They Come Apart* (Carol Stream, IL: Tyndale House Publishers, 2013).

regional differences,[7] political differences,[8] etc. Similar litera-ture is sometimes available about other countries that describes how these or similar dimensions of context play out within those national settings.

Whether engaged in mission domestically or internationally, if you have already identified or established missional relationships, you can often read about the contexts related to those relationships. That might come in the form of a travel guide to Mozambique, a history of Detroit, or a memoir of a formerly homeless person. The details will vary according to your and your church's particular mis-sion engagement, but such descriptive literature often exists and can be an important part of building your understanding.

One technique you may be tempted to use to better under-stand the context in which you conduct mission is a needs assessment. Needs assessments have a long history in mission, social services, and development work. The problem with needs assessments, however, is that they are designed to highlight the negative aspects of a context—its needs. All contexts include both needs and assets—positive elements of a context that can be used for constructive purposes. Instead of a needs assess-ment, consider using a method that seeks to highlight a commu-nity's assets, such as community asset mapping,[9] appreciative inquiry,[10] or a roving listener,[11] so that you can understand the

---

7   Colin Woodard, *American Nations: A History of the Eleven Rival Regional Cultures of North America* (New York: Penguin Books, 2011).

8   Lilliana Mason, *Uncivil Agreement: How Politics Became Our Identity* (Chicago: The University of Chicago Press, 2018).

9   John P. Kretzmann and John L. McKnight, *Building Communities from the Inside Out: A Path Toward Finding and Mobilizing a Community's Assets* (Evanston, IL: The Asset-Based Community Development Insti-tute, Institute for Policy Research, Northwestern University, 1993).

10 "The Center for Appreciative Inquiry," The Center for Appreciative Inquiry, https://www.centerforappreciativeinquiry.net/, visited June 1, 2018.

11 Robert King, "Death and resurrection of an urban church," Faith & Lead-ership, https://www.faithandleadership.com/death-and-resurrection-urban -church, visited June 1, 2018.

positive elements of the contexts in which your mission occurs. That will give you a more well-rounded understanding of the context that will make mutual, give-and-take relationships easier to foster.

Listen, Participate, Observe

No amount of reading or study can substitute for the learning that occurs through listening, participating, and observing. Listening to those with whom we are in mission is *the* primary way to understand how they see the world and how that view of the world ties in to elements of their situation in life, that is, their context. Listen to people's opinions. Listen to their stories. Listen to what they tell you about themselves and their surroundings. Listen to what they *don't* say. When we engage in this type of active listening, it is important to listen not just to the face value of what is said or left unsaid. It is also important to listen to what's behind what is said and what is not said.

Active listening involves asking reflective questions, so go ahead and ask your mission partners to help you understand them better! It's okay to ask people to clarify or explain something that you don't understand, as long as you do it in a respectful way. Most people will be pleased and honored when you show that you are interested in them and care about them by asking questions for the sake of understanding.

Sometimes it may be more appropriate to ask questions after an experience or interaction rather than during it. Waiting until afterward can avoid unintentional confrontation or shaming that could disrupt the experience or interaction as it is happening. Moreover, it may be that you develop one or two trusted people from a context with whom you can ask deeper questions about that context. It may not be appropriate to ask all questions to all people in a particular context. It is important to respect others and their cultural assumptions about what sorts of questions should be asked when, where, and to whom. Yet don't let fear of offending hold you back from asking or an initial unsatisfactory response discourage you from continuing to ask. There will be mistakes and challenges on both sides but keep asking to understand.

Finally, participate in other contexts and observe as you do so. Eat the food. Join in the festivals. Shop at local businesses. Attend meetings. When you're there, look to see who else is there. What are they doing in these places? With whom are they doing it? How are they dressed, how do they talk, and how do they carry themselves? If you are into journaling, it may help to keep a journal of your observations so that you can continue to refer back to them as you learn more about the contexts in which you are in mission.

Observe as much as you can without trying to determine if what you are seeing is "good' or "bad." If you want to learn, suspend your judgment and just watch. You can note your own emotional reactions, since this may help clue you into important differences. But don't assume that your emotional responses are all you need to know about another context. There may come a time when it is necessary to make certain judgments, but if you focus first on observing and understanding, then such judgments can be the result of thoughtful reflection rather than immediate emotional reactions to difference.

Once you've finished observing (for the time being), process what you've seen with someone else. It's best if that processing can happen with someone from that context who can help you understand what you've seen and experienced. This is another chance to ask questions. But even if it's with another person from your home context in mission with you, there is a lot of value in talking through what you've seen with someone else to try to come to a better understanding of what happened, why, and what that tells you about the contexts you are learning about.

Learning another context is an ongoing process. Contexts are complex, multifaceted and always changing. We are never done learning a context, whether that's our own or that of a mission partner. We should not be daunted by the ongoing nature of this task, however. Reading the Bible or praying to get to know God better is also an ongoing process, but we recognize its value and joy! May we treat the process of getting to know ourselves and others better with similar dedication and joy.

■ MISSION TAKEAWAYS

This chapter has introduced a new term to help us think about our differences—context—and explored how to understand our differences better in a variety of theoretical and practical ways. What are the main principles that we should apply to our mission practice from this discussion of contexts? We can identify three takeaways:

1. Context refers to the "world" that people inhabit. That world is shaped by many factors—culture, language, race, gender, class, age, family system, political system, economic system, history, and others. There are also multiple dimensions to an individual's context—organizational, local, national, and international.

2. Context has important implications for how we form relationships with others across difference and how we understand and communicate about the gospel. Therefore, it is important to pay attention to contextual differences between ourselves and those with whom we are in mission. While we should not treat differences as absolute, neither should we ignore them.

3. Understanding contextual differences begins with understanding one's own context. As one becomes more aware of one's own context, one can also start to understand others' contexts, especially through active, receptive engagement with them. The process of learning is ongoing and should be focused on understanding, not judging.

■ DISCUSSION QUESTIONS

Use these questions to guide group study of this chapter or for individual reflection:

1. What words would you use to describe your church context, your family context?

2. What aspects of your context are most important to your sense of who you are? What aspects of your context do you think have had the greatest impact in leading you to your present situation in life?

3. Think of someone who sees the world differently than you do (politically, religiously, in terms of values, etc.). Can you think of any contextual differences between yourself and that person that are associated with the difference(s) in how you see the world?

4. Have you ever miscommunicated with someone because of differences in context? What was the nature of that miscommunication? How was it resolved (if at all)?

5. Think about your or your congregation's current mission involvement. What do you know about the contexts of those with whom you are in mission? How did you learn about those contexts? What have you learned from your mission partners about their contexts?

6. Think about your or your congregation's current mission involvement. What contextual differences exist between you and your congregation on the one hand and those with whom you are in mission on the other? How do these differences affect your relationships with your mission partners? Do these differences create differences in understanding God's good news between you and those with whom you are in mission?

7. Think about your current mission involvement. How might you learn more from your mission partners about their contexts? What types of questions would you need

to ask them? What types of experiences would you need to participate in and observe?

8. Think about any possible new missional relationships identified in the discussion questions from last chapter. How can you incorporate learning about contexts into developing those relationships?

◼ FURTHER READINGS

Here are some other books related to topics in this chapter and why you should read them:

Erin Meyer, *The Culture Map: Decoding How People Think, Lead, and Get Things Done Across Cultures* (New York: Public Affairs, 2014). Meyer examines eight dimensions of cultural difference that can impact how people work together across national backgrounds. The book is written for a business audience but has wider applicability.

Stan Nussbaum, *American Cultural Baggage: How to Recognize and Deal with It* (Maryknoll, NY: Orbis Books, 2005). Nussbaum helps readers understand the values held by American culture through examining a series of common sayings. This book is a useful tool for Americans seeking to understand the cultural part of their context.

Ruby K. Payne, Philip DeVol, and Terie Dreussi Smith, *Bridges Out of Poverty: Strategies for Professionals and Communities* (Highlands, TX: aha! Process, Inc., 2001). Payne and her coauthors present the framework she has developed for understanding the impact class differences make on how people behave and understand the world. She recommends an approach to working with the poor that is based on recognizing these differences and on developing relationships.

Debby Irving, *Waking Up White: And Finding Myself in the Story of Race* (Cambridge, MA: Elephant Room Press, 2014).

Irving shares her personal story of how a lack of awareness and understanding of her white context hampered her efforts to address problems of racism, poverty, and inequality. When she began to examine the assumptions and attitudes she had inherited from her white context, it allowed her to better understand racial difference and engage more authentically and graciously with people from other racial contexts.

6   Transformative Conversations

"What I mean is that we can mutually encourage each other while I am with you. We can be encouraged by the faithfulness we find in each other, both your faithfulness and mine." (Romans 1:12)

Bridges, Gift Giving, and Cross-Pollination

This book has shown thus far that mission involves good news, forming relationships across boundaries, taking the differences involved seriously, and having conversations about God's good news that draw on these differences. This chapter will explore further how such conversations about God's good news happen. To introduce that discussion, though, let's consider three additional metaphors for mission.

Bridges

The first metaphor is missionaries as **bridges**. Christians in mission are not just border crossers between two different territories. Mission does involve crossing boundaries. It involves going into different social settings and perhaps even different countries. Yet missionaries are called to be more than boundary crossers.

They are called to be bridge builders. Bridges are structures that allow travel and transportation across boundaries, whether those boundaries are water, railroad tracks, or another road. Bridges let vehicles, people, and goods travel back and forth. Similarly, missionaries are called to help establish communication, exchange, and understanding between different groups. They bring some insights from their home context into the context of those with whom they are in mission, but they also allow for some insights from the context of those with whom they are in mission to flow back to their home contexts. The exchange goes both ways and, in the process, enriches both sides.

Gift Giving

Missionaries, however, are not just a medium to facilitate exchange. They are involved in that exchange themselves. Therefore, another metaphor for mission is **gift giving**. In gift giving, two (or more) people share something of value to each other. Good gifts are meaningful both to the person giving them and the person receiving them. When I give my daughter Lego building blocks, she is excited to receive them because she loves to play with them, and I am excited to give them because they connect me to her and to my own childhood. Those involved in mission give gifts (of good news) to those with whom they are in mission. Ideally, those gifts are meaningful both to the givers and the mission partners. If the mission partners are uninterested in the gifts, they are not good gifts. Yet mission is not one-sided. It is reciprocal gift giving. Our mission partners also give us gifts. We must recognize those gifts and appreciate their meaning so that our partners can give good gifts as well. If we do not allow others to give us gifts or if we reject or devalue the other's gifts, that harms the relationship.

Cross-Pollination

Gifts can be used or they can be put on a shelf, even when they are treasured. The best mission involves not just an exchange of things to possess or put on a shelf, but an exchange that changes both sides in fruitful ways. In this regard, mission is like **cross-pollination** in plants. In cross-pollination, plants exchange pollen to fertilize each other. This exchange of pollen is the only way that these plants can bear fruit. There are a variety of ways in which pollen is carried from one plant to another, including wind. When we engage in mission, we open ourselves to the wind of the Holy Spirit, share the seeds of good news that we have, and receive seeds of good news from others, all so that we can mutually bear fruit. This fruit will have characteristics from both plants involved. The fruits of our mission partnership are shaped by contributions from both us and our mission partners.

Becoming Conversant

All three of the metaphors above suggest mutual exchange, a process of give and take, a back and forth. The definition of mission which we have been examining throughout this book, which involves conversation, suggests the same. You can't have a true conversation if only one person is talking, or if one person is not listening when the other person talks. True conversation only happens when both sides talk and both sides listen.

Thinking of mission in this mutual way is a challenge for many Christians engaged in mission. Whether we think of mission as helping or mission as evangelism, there is a tendency for Western Christians to think of mission as a one-sided process. All too often, the attitude of Western Christians to their mission partners is "We have money, schools, medicine, etc., which we will give to you. We have the right understanding of God, which we will give to you. We do not need to receive anything from you."

To see mission in this one-sided way is to misunderstand mission for a whole host of reasons. To be in mission, we must be willing to listen and receive, not merely talk and give. Listening and receiving recognizes the worth of others and the assets that others have. It affirms the genuineness of our relationship with them. It even helps us better understand the work God is doing and calls us to do in mission.

Listening to others recognizes the ability they have to discern the ways in which God is at work in their contexts (and perhaps ours, too!). Because mission begins with God, not with us Christians, God is already at work in all contexts before any missionaries show up. Missionaries never bring God to a context; they always go to join in what God is already doing.

Especially when our mission partners are Christians (which they often are, both domestically and abroad), we should expect them to have the same ability to perceive God's action in the world as we do. Their level of material wealth, health, education, etc. in no way limits their ability to perceive God at work. The ability to perceive God is a spiritual ability, not an economic or social ability. Indeed, sometimes being more vulnerable or marginalized allows people to notice God in ways that those who are distracted with security or privilege overlook. One's economic or social standing does not indicate one's standing with God.

Even when those with whom we are in mission are not Christian, we may fairly expect them to have some ability to perceive the actions of God, especially when we encourage them to look. John Wesley believed that God, through prevenient grace, enabled all people to have some ability, no matter how small, to perceive God's gracious action in the world and in their own souls. According to Wesley, it is this grace-given ability to apprehend God that allows people to respond to God's gracious love. Because as Wesleyans we believe in God's prevenient grace, we may also therefore believe that even non-Christians may have something worthwhile to say about what God is doing in the world. That doesn't mean we have to agree with everything that they might say; however, we should not automatically discount everything that they say, either.

Regardless of assets, privilege, or religious affiliation and belief, we should expect everyone to have a unique view of God and God's actions in the world that will be different than our own.

This conclusion follows because everyone's view of God is shaped by his or her unique life experiences and by his or her particular context, as Andrew Walls's theater metaphor, discussed in the last chapter, highlighted. Others will have a different view of the play of God's redemptive action than we do. While others may not be able to see God in some of the same ways we do, they will also be able to see God in ways that we cannot. Thus, there are things we will have missed about God and God's action that they will have seen from where they are sitting. We can learn from those insights.

Of course, conversation depends upon our contribution as well. Listening all the time is no more of a conversation than talking all the time is. Thus, it is important for us to be able to share with our mission partners where we see God at work, what we think is good, and how we want to see the world renewed. If we are asking others about their understandings of God and their contexts, it is natural for us to share our own understandings as part of the back and forth of a natural conversation.

When we discuss with others, though, it is important that we treat these interactions as conversations and not as debates. In a debate, there are two opposing sides, and the goal of each side is to prove that it is right, and the other side is wrong. A conversation is very different than a debate. First of all, a conversation does not presume opposing sides. There are participants in a conversation, not sides. Participants in a conversation cooperate; they are not opponents. Differences of opinion may arise in the course of conversation, and participants in the conversation may argue for the correctness of their views or critique the views of others, but this is not the main point of a conversation. A successful conversation is not one in which you persuade someone that you are right; a successful conversation is one in which all participants walk away feeling heard in the interaction, feeling good about their relationship, and perhaps feeling like they've gotten something of value from the conversation. When we share our understandings through our verbal interactions with others, we should do so in this spirit of mutual conversation, not in the spirit of monologue or debate.

In Word and Deed

Thus far, I have mostly described mission as conversation instead of as action. In part, I have taken this approach because I think Methodists (and especially American Methodists) jump too quickly to action. (See chapter 4.) Our orientation toward action is part of our theological (and cultural) DNA. Speaking of mission as conversation reminds us that there is more to mission than doing. Mission is being in relationship.

And in part, I've taken this approach to describing mission because even when mission does involve doing, I think that conversation provides an important metaphor for how we understand the actions we do. Mission certainly involves action, but it helps us if we think about those actions as an embodied form of conversation.

Thus, when we act in mission, we are making a statement with our actions about where we see God at work, what we see as good, how we hope to renew the world, and thus ultimately a statement about how we understand God's good news. When we plant trees to care for the earth, we proclaim the hope of a renewed earth where life can flourish. When we visit the imprisoned, we witness to a God who forgives sins and doesn't let people's misdeeds be the last word about their lives and worth. When we support a community in developing its health infrastructure, we enact the good news of Jesus's healing. Actions, therefore, can be an important part of the conversation of mission.

Yet even when we act out part of our conversation about good news, it is important to talk directly as well. Talking is necessary for several reasons. First, without discussion (and even sometimes with), it is possible that others will perceive a different message in our actions than the one that we intend to send. We may think that we are conveying love, but others may see it as contempt or a desire for control. To use a benign example, a family member thought that she was showing love by cooking macaroni and cheese every time another family member came over, because she assumed the guest loved her macaroni and cheese. Really, they didn't like the dish that much, and she was just setting it up so that everyone would eat the same unwanted meal repeatedly. Yet she never asked what they wanted to eat, and they never felt comfortable telling her they didn't like her macaroni and cheese. Without talking, there was no way to clarify what was going on. This sort of dialogue with others is important because it can lead us to change our actions in mission to be more effective, or at least how we carry them out so that the messages we intend to convey through our actions come through more clearly.

Second, our actions are not listening. Our actions may show what *we* believe about God and God's good news, but they tell us nothing about what *others* think about God's good news. We must still listen to others for there to be a conversation. Sometimes that can involve paying attention to others' actions, too. If our actions are a way of embodying conversation, then we should regard others' actions in the same way. We should pay attention to what they do and how they act when we are together in mission. These actions can give important clues about what and how our mission partners think, which they might not share through their words. Yet despite the helpfulness of watching others' actions, listening must involve listening to their words as well. Otherwise we run the same risk of misunderstanding the meaning behind their actions as they run of misunderstanding ours. Talking is important for clarifying the meaning of actions, both ours and our mission partners'.

Money Talks

There is another danger in the part of our conversations we carry out through our actions, and that danger comes from the impact of money. There is an American saying that "money talks." This saying indicates that those with more money are often given a larger voice in conversations and greater influence in deciding what actions are done. Since much action in mission, especially that organized in a traditional, programmatic fashion, requires money, those willing to donate money to mission have historically been able to determine what actions and what programs happen.

While generosity is good, and while the wealthy should have an opportunity to participate in conversations just like everyone else, this tie between donating and decision-making has some serious implications for our mission conversations. If we are not careful, money will talk, and it will drown out other voices. The monetarily poor may be unwilling to speak up or to challenge the monetarily rich for fear that if they contradict or offend the rich, they will withhold their money from that mission partnership. Thus, the monetarily poor have an economic incentive to tell the monetarily rich what they want to hear, so that they will feel good and continue to give money, rather than what may be real about a situation, project, or opinion. In this way, money can create inequalities that warp and stifle conversation. Moreover, it can undermine self-determination by the monetarily poor. In order to receive vital financial and physical resources, the monetarily poor are forced to accept the decision-making of the monetarily rich.

There are several ways to address and confront the distorting effects money can have on our mission partnerships. First, when we are acting out the conversation of mission, it is important that these actions be in the model of "doing with" rather than "doing for." "Doing with" implies partnership and shared decision-making, whereas "doing for" implies that the one initiating the action is making all the decisions.

Mission Roundtables

There are specific models for how to collaboratively plan joint actions in the vein of "doing with." One important model is mission roundtables. The goal of mission roundtables is to create a structured space wherein ground rules and shared expectations help all partners participate freely. Roundtables seek to recognize the assets that each partner brings to collaborative work. While some partners bring monetary and other economic assets, other partners will bring other forms of assets—knowledge, skills, relationships, networks, and spiritual insights. Roundtables depend upon recognizing that all assets have value and may be necessary for a project to happen.

Money as an Expression of Love

Not letting money dominate the conversation also involves changes of attitudes and the cultivation of trust. First, it requires that those with more money not insist that their way prevail. It requires that their generosity not be contingent on them getting their way, but rather is given freely as an expression of their love. Again, that doesn't mean they should have no say in how their money is used, but it might mean that they commit to their generosity before plans for its use are finalized. It certainly means that those with more money must be willing to listen to those with less money, value their decision-making ability, and be willing to adjust their own thinking accordingly.

Creating Space

Such a shift also involves a change in thinking by mission partners who are monetarily poor. Because the notion that the monetarily rich make decisions is deeply ingrained in the structure of mission (and secular aid) and has been for centuries, mission partners with less money have often internalized the notion that they must be silent and deferential to those with more money. To shift the dynamics, they must be willing to speak up. Yet that burden is not entirely on them. Creating space for the voices of the monetarily poor and affirming rather than immediately critiquing those voices when raised are important behaviors by the monetarily rich that can support the poor in raising their voice.

Ultimately, those with less money will feel more comfortable in speaking up when there is trust between all partners. The need for trust again points to the relational nature of mission.

Relationships, and the trust that comes from relationships, are key to allowing mutual conversation.

People, God, Context

Thus far, I have talked about conversation as taking place between two sets of participants—us and our mission partners. This two-sided model needs expanding, though, for two reasons. First, we should not presume that all of our mission partners have the same things to contribute to a conversation. Nor should we assume, when a group of Christians goes out in mission, that each of those being sent has the same things to contribute to a conversation. Each person involved in mission has their own unique contribution to make to the conversation, whether missionary or mission partner.

Second, the conversation of mission does not just take place between people. The conversation of mission is also a conversation with God and with human contexts. God is an important part of the conversation because the conversation is about *God's* good news. If we want to know more about God's good news, then we should be willing to listen to God and share our understandings, hopes, fears, and confusions with God. The conversation is also a conversation about the meaning of God's good news *in particular contexts*. Thus, we need to pay attention to how our mission partners' contexts and our own contexts shape the conversation in ways that go beyond the viewpoints of particular individuals.

The conversation of mission always begins with God.

The conversation of mission always begins with God. We saw in chapter 1 how mission begins with God's sending, initially with God's sending of Godself to the world in the form of Jesus. In the Incarnation, Jesus entered into human contexts for the sake of engaging humans in conversation in word and deed about God's good news. Since mission is first and foremost God's mission, the conversation of mission always starts with God and God's Incarnate Word in Jesus Christ.

Conversing with God in mission can happen in a variety of ways, but two primary ones are prayer and Bible study. Prayer is our direct way of talking with God. Prayer involves our sharing with God, and that sharing can include our thoughts and feelings about our mission work. When you are engaged in mission, you should be praying about that mission. Yet prayer is also our way of listening to God. When we pray about our mission, we must also include time to be still and listen for the voice of God and the leading of the Holy Spirit.

Bible study is another important way for us to hear God's voice in our mission conversations. The Bible contains "all things necessary to salvation" and is "the true rule and guide for faith and practice."[1] Thus, it presents God's voice to us. Yet to truly hear God's voice through the Bible, we must be prepared to really wrestle with the Bible, to ask questions of it, to be honest about how we understand it and where it confuses us. We don't hear God's voice by reciting platitudes about the Bible. We do hear God's voice when we really pay attention to the text, take ownership of the interpretive process, and bring our whole selves to the process of understanding it.

Remember, prayer and Bible study are not just ways that those sent in mission can converse with God; they are ways in which our mission partners can converse with God, too. In fact, there's a lot to be learned, both about our partners and about God, by engaging in prayer and Bible study with our mission partners. Doing so provides a focus to our conversations with our mission partners and thus a means to get to know them, and our mission partners can bring new insights into what God is saying to us as we pray together and discuss the Bible. Of course, our mission partners

---

1   *The Book of Discipline of The United Methodist Church 2016* (Nashville: The United Methodist Publishing House, 2016), 66, 73.

must be willing to engage in this form of conversation, and not all may be. Nevertheless, we miss out on an important chance for conversation when we fail to even offer the opportunity.

Beyond the human participants and the Divine participant in the mission conversation, it is also a conversation with human contexts. Human contexts are, of course, a product of humanity, but they also transcend individual humans and have perspectives that go beyond the opinions of any individual. Making a lot of money is an important value in American culture, but it is not my personal top priority. In a mission conversation with me, it would be important both to know the cultural norm of my context and my own personal view of that norm.

Thus, when we are engaged in mission conversations, we should also reflect not just on our own individual views but on what the dominant views are in our own contexts. Similarly, we should be asking ourselves not just, "What do our mission partners think?" but "What is the dominant view in our mission partners' context(s)?" Just as we sometimes disagree with our larger contexts, our mission partners will also sometimes disagree with theirs. Even when we or our mission partners disagree with our contexts, we must still decide how to handle that disagreement and negotiate that conflict with others within the context. When we make the distinction between individuals and their contexts, we can think more deeply about where to affirm and where to challenge either individuals or their contexts, while recognizing that the two are separate questions.

Having the Talk

The conversation of mission is thus a conversation between individual humans, God, and human contexts about God's good news and good news in general. What, though, does that conversation actually look like? It is a process of trying to understand how all involved see the goodness and the newness of good news, and how these varying perspectives fit together.

Good news is first of all good—it is positive, life-giving, joy-producing, and beneficial. The Bible has perspectives on what counts as good news, as discussed in chapter 3, and it is important to consider what is good about these versions of good news as part of this conversation. Here, our contexts will impact our perceptions of biblical teachings, since how we understand good news in other areas of our lives will influence how we understand God's good news. Thus, it is important that we be aware of how good news is defined in our contexts so that we can be aware of how we approach scripture.

To understand how others see God's good news, we must also understand what they and their contexts see as good. Here, the views of individuals and the views of their contexts may or may not be the same. We may not agree with those views, individual or context-based, and we may not think that what they see as good is what God would see as good. But if we are going to be in conversation, we need to ask the question, and we need to listen without immediately rushing to judgment. We need to take what they see as good seriously, whether or not we agree. Moreover, we need to be open to the possibility that they may have something to teach us about God's understanding of goodness and how it applies to our own lives and contexts, something that we may not have considered before.

Second, good news is new. It's something different from how the world already is and how the world already works. As we think through the forms of good news listed in chapter 3, we should ask ourselves what is new about these versions of good news. Where do they differ from the world around us? This question can apply either to our own contexts or the contexts of those with whom we are in mission.

A good question for us to ask our mission partners is what their hopes and dreams are, both for themselves as individuals and their broader contexts. How would they like the world to be different than it is? What dreams do they have for themselves, their loved ones, and their communities? What forms of newness do they long for? Again, we may or may not agree with or share these hopes and dreams, and we may or may not think these hopes and dream line up with God's. That's not the immediate point. The initial point is merely to ask, be willing to listen to the answers, and take them seriously for the sake of the conversation. There is plenty of time to weigh the value of others' answers (and our own) as the conversation goes on. Quick judgment shuts down rather than expands conversation. Moreover, when we react with judgment, we shut ourselves off from what we could learn from others about the ways in which God desires to bring newness and change to our own lives and our own home contexts. We have insights to gain from this conversation, too.

Mission, like conversation, is an iterative process, something we do again and again. We say something or do something. Our mission partners say or do something in response. We then respond, perhaps by saying or doing something new, or perhaps by saying or doing the same thing but in a different way. We pray and read the Bible, either by ourselves or with our mission partners, to try to understand God's perspective. We pay attention to the distinction between individual views and those of the wider context. So it goes continually, back and forth. The process doesn't end, though there are insights, breakthroughs, and other significant moments along the way.

Being Real

A final word of caution is in order about how we approach this conversation about God's good news. Although the conversation is about good news, that does not mean we must always present our lives or the lives of Christians in general as being always about happiness, perfection, and success. That is just not true. There are hard times in everyone's life, Christian or not. Everyone has flaws. Everyone has times when they fail. To pretend otherwise does a disservice to our mission partners, to our relationships with them, and to ourselves.

We do a disservice to our mission partners when we are unwilling to share our own weaknesses and vulnerabilities because we present to them a false understanding of good news. God's good news does not mean the end of all our problems or our immediate perfection. In fact, the Bible talks a lot about Christians suffering and about persistent sin among Christians. If we present God's good news without mentioning these continued (and at times even heightened) difficulties, we set our mission partners up for disappointment. Difficulties will come in life, and both our mission partners and we need to have a faith that can withstand and make sense of those difficulties.

Second, we dishonor our relationships with our mission partners if we are not willing to be real with them. If we share only the good aspects of our lives in an attempt to present God's good news, we are not sharing our lives fully. We are withholding something from the relationship, and that can only damage the relationship. When we are not willing to be vulnerable about our own weaknesses, difficulties, failures, and struggles, we are not being fully honest in our conversations. Dishonesty erodes trust, and as noted above, trust is a prerequisite for healthy conversation.

Finally, when we are not honest in our mission conversations about our shortcomings and challenges, we do ourselves a disservice. If we do not make ourselves vulnerable in discussing God's good news with our mission partners, we hide not only from others but from God. By so doing, we shut ourselves off from possibly hearing good news about those very shortcomings and challenges from our mission partners. It may be that God desires to speak good news to us in the midst of our struggles and that God desires to do so through our mission partners. Yet for God to do so, we need to be honest, vulnerable, and real in our conversations with those mission partners.

Mission and Spirituality

The possibility that God may speak good news to us through our mission partners shows just how powerful the practice of mission may be for our spiritual development. That is why Christians should approach mission not as an obligation, but as a central practice of the Christian life, as Chapter 1 argued. Engaging in mission offers us a variety of spiritual benefits.

> **God may give us good news through our mission partners.**

First, when we engage in mission, we grow in humility. Humility means recognizing one's humanness. It's an important spiritual practice. When we have humility, we recognize that we are not God. Because we are not God, we do not know everything about God or God's action in the world. That's okay, because it is only when we recognize the ways in which we do not yet know God that we can come to know and love God better. Ironically, it is when we have humility about the limits of our knowledge of God that we have the greatest opportunities to grow in that knowledge. And engaging in mission conversation often does show us the limits of our knowledge of God. Thus, listening to our mission partners is not only a way to open ourselves up to each other; it's a way to open ourselves up to God.

Second, when we engage in mission, we grow in love. We grow in love for ourselves by growing in humility. As the last chapter discussed, when we learn humility, we are able to forge a self-love that is based on our true identity as beings created in the image of God. This form of self-love is truer and stronger than one based on a false works-righteousness in which we love ourselves because we think we are good enough or successful enough or perfect enough to deserve love. We grow in love for others through mission, too. Our relationships with others through mission have been a central focus of this book. Yet those relationships are characterized not just by familiarity or knowledge or cooperation. They are ultimately characterized by love. Mission allows us to practice loving others, and practice is what helps us get better. Finally, we grow in love for God through mission. As we learn more about God from conversations with our mission partners, that new knowledge about God gives us new reasons to love God. We experience God's good news in new ways, and we love God more for it.

Third, when we engage in mission, we grow in faithful endurance. Mission is a long-term process, but there are still encouragements along the way. In this regard, mission reflects the Wesleyan understanding of sanctification. Sanctification is an ongoing process of growing in love for God and others. The process is never over (or at least very few achieve entire sanctification in this life), but there are still significant milestones and tangible forms of growth along the way. As Wesleyan Christians, we are going on to perfection, but we understand that there is value in the journey and not just the destination. Similarly, we may be working in mission toward the kingdom of God or freedom from sin or new life or fully restored relationships. We long for the destination, yet we understand that there is also value in the journey. God does not expect us to bring about the kingdom completely through our own actions. God does expect us to be faithful in our efforts toward establishing the kingdom, even if we do not get there in this life. We do our part, and trust God to take care of the rest.

Mission Leads to Transformation

When we engage in this sort of mutual, honest, ongoing, conversation in words and deeds about God's good news in and for the world, we should expect transformation to happen. It is not just talk for the sake of talk. Although we are never done being part of God's mission, that doesn't mean that nothing happens or changes as part of God's mission. Remember, God's good news is new! It changes things. When we engage in mission, we join in the work of our God who proclaims, "Look! I'm making all things new" (Revelation 21:5). This newness, this change, involves a process of ongoing transformation, and this transformation happens in several different ways.

First, mission transforms strangers into neighbors and neighbors into friends. We saw in the story of the good Samaritan how the traveler and the Samaritan were transformed from strangers (and even enemies) into friends. This book has argued throughout that building relationships across boundaries is central to mission, not just as a means but as an end. Such relationships transform strangers into friends. They transform separation into connection. This transformation both facilitates discussion of God's good news and is itself a component of that good news. God is a God of reconciliation and relationship, a God of love.

God's good news in mission can also transform our neighbors and their contexts. When someone finds new life in Christ, that is transformation! When someone has a new sense of "somebodiness," because they are accepted into relationship, that is transformation! When small loans and skills training allow women to start businesses and support their families, that is transformation! When diseases are eliminated, that is transformation! When Christians grow in their knowledge of their faith, that is transformation! When our air and water are cleaner because of the mission work we have done, that is transformation! When we engage in mission, it brings transformation both to our neighbors as individuals and to their broader cultural, social, economic, and political contexts. This expectation for both personal and societal change is a deeply Wesleyan way of anticipating the fruits of God's mission.

Yet it is not only our neighbors and our mission partners who are transformed through mission. We are ourselves transformed when we engage in mission. We come to care about those whom we previously disregarded. We see the world in new ways. We understand ourselves and our own contexts in new ways. We feel our faith strengthened and our passion for God increased. We find spiritual and emotional healing. We treat others in our home context differently and in a more Christlike way. We, too, are transformed. And when we are transformed, we become agents of transformation not only while in mission, but in all aspects of our lives. By doing so, we transform our families, our workplaces, our churches, our neighborhoods, our cities, and our countries through our everyday living. Thus, our home contexts can be changed through mission, too.

Furthermore, those sent in mission and those among whom they are in mission are not just transformed separately; they are transformed together. All mission partners are mutually transformed because our collective understanding of God's good news is transformed. God may be the same yesterday, today, and tomorrow, but our human understandings of our eternal God are never full nor complete. We never know enough about God and God's love. Moreover, while God is always the same, God's mercies are new every morning. There is always more to learn about the good news of God's continually new mercy. Finally, God's good news is always good news for people in particular places and times. God has a message for each of us in our place and time, but when we put those messages together, we get glimpses of the bigger picture of God's love for the world.

Thus, when we engage in discussion as mission partners with each other about God's good news, it brings out aspects of the good news that weren't apparent before to all participants. Each participant in missional conversations about God's good news learns to see aspects of good news that another participant could see, but he or she could not. And more than that, the process of interacting and discussing the nature of God's good news allows all participants to see aspects that none of them could see before. The Holy Spirit works through these conversations to impart God's love to us all. And what could be better news than that?

■ MISSION TAKEAWAYS

This chapter has delved into the central metaphor of conversation and also highlighted the spiritual significance of mission. How should these insights shape our mission theoretically, practically, and spiritually? We can identify three takeaways:

1. Share in missional conversation what you think is good and what you think is new (or different from the ways of the world) about God's good news. This sharing can happen through words and actions. Missional conversations require mutual sharing and mutual listening that take the form of dialogue, not debate. Such conversations should extend to learning from God and human contexts as well as mission partners.

2. Beware of forces that can disrupt or distort conversation. In particular, pay attention to the impact of money on conversation, and be honest in conversation about the good and bad in your life and your context. Focus on building trust, as it is necessary to support genuine, healthy conversations.

3. Mission leads to transformation. When you engage in mission, don't just expect your mission partners to be transformed or the world to be transformed. Expect to be transformed yourself. Expect that you and your mission partners' mutual understanding of God and God's good news will be transformed. In this way, you will experience the spiritual benefit of practicing mission as a central part of the Christian life.

■ DISCUSSION QUESTIONS

Use these questions to guide group study of this chapter or for individual reflection:

1. Which of the metaphors for mission (bridge, gift giving, cross-pollination) described at the opening of this chapter resonates most with you? Why?

2. When you think about what God's good news means to you, what is good about it? What is new (or different from how the world works) about it? How might you convey that good news in words or demonstrate it in actions to someone else?

3. When you think about listening to others' understanding of God's good news, what might be some challenges for you personally to listening to your mission partners? What might be some challenges for your church as a whole?

4. This chapter said there is a need to be real and vulnerable in our mission conversations. How do you respond? Do you agree? What might be scary or challenging about opening yourself up in this way? What is exciting?

5. Thinking about your church's current and past mission involvement, who or what has been transformed through that mission? Was this transformation lasting? Is it ongoing?

6. As you think about the future of your and your church's mission involvement, what would it mean to be prepared for transformation, even if you cannot predict ahead of time what that transformation might look like? How can you open yourself up to transformation by the Holy Spirit through mission?

7. Thinking about your own personal involvement in mission, how has this involvement impacted your faith? Has your faith been transformed in any way through mission? What spiritual benefits have you derived from mission?

▉ FURTHER READING

Here are some other books related to topics in this chapter and why you should read them:

E. Stanley Jones, *The Christ of the Indian Road* (various editions). Jones was one of the greatest Methodist missionaries of all times. In this classic book, first published in 1925, he recounts how his mission work in India changed him and his understanding of the gospel and how his discussions with leading Indian thinkers helped draw him to a deeper understanding of Christ and Christianity.

Vincent Donovan, *Christianity Rediscovered, 25th anniversary edition* (Maryknoll, NY: Orbis Books, 2003). Donovan was a Catholic priest who worked among the Masai people of Kenya. Through conversations with them and by coming to understand the world through their eyes, he came to see that for them to embrace the Christian faith, they needed to be able understand it on their terms, not his. This realization changed Donovan's faith as well.

Sara Miles, *Take This Bread: A Radical Conversion* (New York: Ballantine Books, 2007). Miles shares the story of her conversion from atheism to a Christian faith centered on food: sharing communion and sharing meals by starting a series of food pantries. For her, food becomes a means of divine love, a way of forming relationships with people, even unlikely relationships with those different from her in many ways.

Gregory Boyle, *Tattoos on the Heart: The Power of Boundless Compassion* (New York: Free Press, 2010). Boyle is a Catholic priest and runs Homeboy Industries, a rehabilitation program for ex-gang members in Los Angeles. In this book, he recounts what he has learned about compassion and recognizing our common humanity from those with whom he works.

Laceye Warner and Gaston Warner, *From Relief to Empowerment: How Your Church Can Cultivate Sustainable Mission* (Nashville: Wesley's Foundery Books, 2018). Using the example of ZOE, a nonprofit organization that empowers over twenty-eight thousand orphans and children in seven countries across three continents, including Africa, India, and Guatemala, the Warners argue that mission flourishes when relationships are characterized by mutuality. While there are times for the relief efforts and traditional charity when disasters strike, if years later the same people are receiving the same aid, an opportunity is lost. Mission that moves beyond relief to empowerment opens up ways to address systemic forms of oppression and poverty.

CPSIA information can be obtained
at www.ICGtesting.com
Printed in the USA
LVHW110851011220
673036LV00011B/2329

9 781945 935473